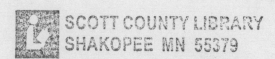

HITCHCOCK
in Hollywood

Of Related Interest from Continuum

American History/American Film, New Expanded Edition, John E. O'Connor and Martin A. Jackson, eds.

American History/American Television, John E. O'Connor, ed.

And the Winner Is . . . The History and Politics of the Oscar Awards, New Expanded Edition, Emanuel Levy

The Cinema of Stanley Kubrick, New Expanded Edition, Norman Kagan

The Dead that Walk: Dracula, Frankenstein, the Mummy, and other Favorite Movie Monsters, Leslie Halliwell

Framework: A History of Screenwriting in the American Film, New Expanded Edition, Tom Stempel

The French through Their Films, Robin Buss

Hitchcock: The First Forty-Four Films, Eric Rohmer and Claude Chabrol

Italian Cinema: From Neorealism to the Present, New Expanded Edition, Peter Bondanella

Loser Take All: The Comic Art of Woody Allen, New Expanded Edition, Maurice Yacowar

A Project for the Theatre, Ingmar Bergman

The Screening of America: Movies and Values from Rocky *to* Rain Man, Tom O'Brien

Screening Space: The American Science Fiction Film, Vivian Sobchack

Small-Town America in Film: The Decline and Fall of Community, Emanuel Levy

Steven Spielberg: The Man, His Movies, and Their Meaning, Philip M. Taylor

Storytellers to the Nation: A History of American Television Writing, Tom Stempel

Take 22: Moviemakers on Moviemaking, Judith Crist

Teleliteracy: Taking Television Seriously, David Bianculli

Toms, Coons, Mulattoes, Mammies, and Bucks: An Interpretive History of Blacks in American Films, New Expanded Edition, Donald Bogle

World Cinema since 1945: An Encyclopedic History, William Luhr, ed.

For more information on these and other titles on the performing arts or literature, write to:

The Continuum Publishing Company
370 Lexington Avenue
New York, NY 10017

HITCHCOCK
in Hollywood

JOEL W. FINLER

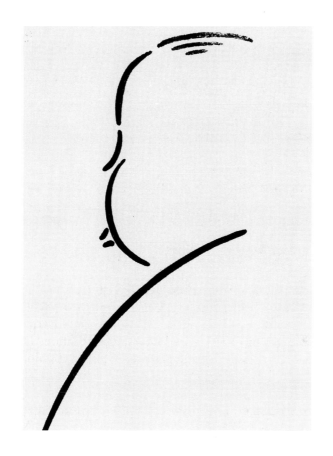

CONTINUUM/NEW YORK

Dedicated to Barbara G.
with love

1992
The Continuum Publishing Company
370 Lexington Avenue, New York, NY 10017

Copyright © 1992 by Joel M. Finler

Printed in Great Britain

Library of Congress Cataloging-in-Publication Data

Finler, Joel W. (Joel Waldo)
    Hitchcock in Hollywood / Joel W. Finler.
        p.   cm.
    Includes bibliographical references and index.
    ISBN 0-8264-0616-5 (hardcover)
    1. Hitchcock, Alfred, 1899– —Criticism and interpretation.
    I. Title.
    PN1998.3.H58F55   1992
    791.43'0233'092—dc20   92–12202
                                                              CIP

Contents

1

Introduction

> If Hitchcock, to my way of thinking, outranks the rest, it is because he is the most complete film-maker of all. He is not merely an expert at some specific aspect of cinema, but an all-round specialist who excels at every image, each shot and every scene. He masterminds the construction of the screenplay as well as the photography, the cutting and the soundtrack, has creative ideas on everything and can handle anything and is even expert at publicity! (François Truffaut)

Alfred Hitchcock, the 'master of suspense', is one of the most remarkable figures in the history of the cinema. He became closely identified with the thriller or suspense movie relatively early in his career, when such pictures were generally looked down on by more serious film-makers and moviegoers. Hitchcock was quick to recognize and exploit the serious possibilities of the genre. His best pictures work on many levels; technically polished, with gripping and suspenseful plots, witty dialogue and often featuring top stars, they have an immediate appeal to audiences. He used the popular thriller format as a means of probing deep into the fears, foibles and neuroses of modern man. His films are full of surprises.

Generally uninterested in the activities of professional criminals or gangsters, he was fascinated by psychologically disturbed characters, both male and female, and enjoyed using his star actors in different and unexpected ways.

In their first film together, he made Cary Grant an embezzler, liar and possible murderer in *Suspicion* (1941); the sophisticated Joseph Cotten played a serial killer in *Shadow of a Doubt* (1943), while the heroine in *Psycho* (1960), played by Janet Leigh, is a thief on the run who is killed off less than half-way through the picture. Acquiring the services of Sean Connery, fresh from his early success as James Bond, Hitchcock cast him in the role of a sensitive, caring and complex hero in *Marnie* (1964).

Similarly, he provided Robert Walker, the handsome young MGM star, with the best role of his career as a homicidal psychopath in *Strangers on a Train* (1951).

Hitchcock often presents us with attractive heroes or heroines who are troubled by serious psychological problems – Gregory Peck in *Spellbound* (1945), the obsessive James Stewart in *Vertigo* (1958) and Tippi Hedren in *Marnie* – leading to unexpected complications. Thus, many of his films emerge as cautionary tales – about the dangers of falling in love with, and attempting to sort out the psychological problems of a wanted murderer (*Spellbound*) or of a compulsive lady thief (*Marnie*), or the risks involved in spying on one's neighbours (*Rear Window*, 1954), or in spending the night alone in an isolated motel (*Psycho*).

With his characteristically wicked sense of humour, Hitchcock was fond of placing his characters under stress, in unfamiliar surroundings, and observing their insecurities. We are led to identify with the handsome, middle-class heroes played by Robert Donat in *The 39 Steps* (1935) and Cary Grant in *North by Northwest* (1959) who suddenly find themselves wanted for murder and on the run from the real murderers as well as the police, forced to use their wits to survive. We are similarly caught up in the problems of the tennis-playing hero (Farley Granger) of *Strangers on a Train*, suspected of the murder of his wife after a chance encounter and subsequent involvement with a psychopathic murderer, and with the wealthy, bored heroine (Tippi Hedren) of *The Birds* (1963), who suddenly finds herself and her boyfriend's family under attack for no apparent reason.

In addition, many of Hitchcock's best films are memorable for their unconventional villains. He is fond of presenting them as attractive, even charismatic, figures and takes special care to make them fully developed and interesting characters. Beginning with Joseph Cotten (*Shadow of a Doubt*) and Claude Rains (*Notorious*, 1946), this tradition was carried on in the 1950s by Robert Walker in *Strangers on a Train*, James Mason in *North by Northwest* and Anthony Perkins in *Psycho*.

Although Hitchcock is best remembered today as a leading figure in Hollywood, he had previously made his name in the 1930s as the outstanding British director of thrillers. Beginning with *The Man Who Knew Too Much* (1934) and *The 39 Steps* he demonstrated a special mastery of the technique with which he has become identified over the years – the shifts between objective and subjective viewpoint that serve to involve the film audience with his leading characters, his attention to atmosphere and detail and his ability with actors. He was known for the care and attention that he put into his scripts and for his meticulous pre-production planning. When he arrived in the US and began making his films for a worldwide audience, with famous stars and more generous budgets, working with leading producers (David Selznick, Walter Wanger) and writers (Ben Hecht, Thornton Wilder), he found that a greater attention to story values and narrative coherence, and a fuller exploration of character and psychology, could easily be accommodated within his already established style. His special personal qualities and inventiveness and especially his strong visual sense continued to be a feature of his post-1939 films.

Hitchcock was one of a group of new directors who made their mark on Hollywood in the early 1940s. He was quickly successful and played an important role, along with other, already established directors, in helping to upgrade the status of director from contract employee to the more independent position of producer-director, with a larger degree of creative control over his projects.

In addition, Hitchcock benefited from the fact that he was so closely identified with suspense or thriller movies at a time when leading directors and stars were showing more serious interest in this genre than ever before. Here, too, he was influential, helping to give this area of film-making a new, mainstream respectability. As Christopher Wicking has suggested,

> If Welles was a somewhat peripheral father-figure of the thriller, Hitchcock remains its presiding genius. The 1940s saw him turn to Hollywood and employ the craft of American cinema – its enormous professionalism and technical skill – to reach artistic maturity . . . Hitchcock's reputation as a master film maker, and his new success in America, undoubtedly helped to make the thriller more respectable within the industry during the 1940s. (*Anatomy of the Movies*, ed. David Pirie)

Though Hitchcock had a brief period at the end of that decade when he was less successful, he recovered quickly in the early 1950s, moving to Paramount in 1953, where he began the most productive and celebrated years of his career. It was just around this time that the French critics at the magazine *Cahiers du Cinéma* became especially interested in his films. As aspiring directors themselves, they were naturally attracted to one whom they recognized as a 'complete film-maker' and a kind of cinematic *auteur*. An additional appeal was the fact that he had generally been neglected by other critics at the time; perhaps his very success had led most critics to regard him as merely a popular entertainer whose films were not worthy of serious discussion. But the French were intrigued by what they saw as the thematic richness of his *oeuvre*. Since Hitchcock had always endeavoured to avoid repeating himself, he had made a wide variety of films within the suspense and thriller genre.

Thus, there was a special appeal to writing about him, examining, for example, the ways in which he had developed and reworked many of his favourite themes and plot lines.

A special Hitchcock edition of *Cahiers du Cinéma*, which appeared in October 1954, was followed by Eric Rohmer and Claude Chabrol's fascinating and provocative monograph on Hitchcock in 1957. Paying special attention to Catholic themes of guilt and innocence, which they discovered running through many of his films, they were particularly intrigued by the exchange or transfer of guilt that often takes place when an otherwise innocent character is unwittingly made the accomplice to a crime. Such themes could be traced back to Hitchcock's earliest successes of the 1920s – *The Lodger* (1926) and *Blackmail* (1929) – up to the 1950s with *Strangers on a Train* and *I Confess* (1952) and even allowed Rohmer and Chabrol to conclude their book with reference to *The Man Who Knew Too Much* (1956) and *The Wrong Man* (1956).

Hitch seen here on the set of his first part-talkie, *Blackmail*, in 1929 with his Czech-born star, Anny Ondra, whose accent was so bad that her voice had to be dubbed by an English actress. This production still shows the problems faced by film-makers at the beginning of the talkie era when the camera had to be enclosed in a sound-proof booth.

Another future film-maker, Peter Bogdanovich, compiled a mono-graph on Hitchcock for the Museum of Modern Art in 1963. François Truffaut's full-length interview book first appeared in French in 1966 and in English the following year and has been rightly regarded ever since as a basic source on the director's career. The rapid growth in the number of books and magazines on the cinema was further stimulated by the boom in university film courses and film departments, especially in the US, during the late 1960s and 1970s. Here, too, Hitchcock was a much favoured subject. In England alone there were numerous articles and interviews (especially in *Movie* magazine), Robin Wood's 'Hitch-cock's Films' appeared in 1965 and Ray Durgnat's series on 'The Strange Case of Alfred Hitchcock' was first published in *Films & Filming* in 1970, followed by an expanded version in book form. These were but the first in a veritable flood of writings on Hitchcock that continued throughout the 1970s and 1980s.

Though there have been two major biographies (John Russell Taylor and Donald Spoto) and a book on his relationship with Selznick in the 1940s (Leff), the vast majority of the writing has been devoted to analys-ing the films in ever greater depth and detail, and from a variety of new critical viewpoints – ideological, feminist, Marxist, etc. – filtered through semiotics and structuralism. Unfortunately far too much of the writing has been by academics for other academics or film students, published by scholarly magazines or university presses. All too often the books or articles written by lecturers in film or cultural studies demonstrate a background knowledge in theatre and literature, but little understanding of the film-making process and little knowledge of, or interest in, the history of Hollywood or the workings of the American film industry.

There appears to be a serious gap here between the analytical studies of Hitchcock and his films, on one hand, and the biographical writing that presents useful information about his life and film-making, but suffers from a lack of historical perspective. Regarding myself as a film historian, rather than a 'critic', with a special interest in, and familiarity with, the development of the American cinema, in this book I shall be attempting to fill that gap.

Since Hitchcock is widely regarded as the archetype of the successful producer-director, it is surprising that so little attention has been paid to such questions as: how he became so successful (and famous) in Holly-wood so quickly; how he was able to sustain and develop his career for such a long period of time; whether he had any flops (he did) and how he recovered from them. Also, what was the relationship between the artistic or critical success or failure of his films, and success or failure at the box office?

There is now more information available than ever before on Hitchcock's creative approach to film-making and his working methods; on the budgets, costs and profits of individual films; on his relationship with producers, writers and other collaborators; on how he dealt with various technical challenges, experimenting with extremely long takes, the changeover from black-and-white to colour and widescreen filming.

Since Hitchcock was such a complete film-maker, involved in every aspect of his films, any analytical discussion that fails to consider the relevant production details and the nature of his collaboration with writers, designers, cameramen and others within a more general understanding of his particular approach to film-making is also likely to misrepresent the films themselves. In an effort to gain a fuller understanding of Hitchcock and his films and make sense of his development as a filmmaker, I have attempted to assemble this information into, I hope, a new and more meaningful pattern, dealing with the individual pictures within the context of his American career as a whole, while also placing him within the development of the American cinema from the time of his arrival in Hollywood in 1939 up to the mid-1960s in particular, his most active and successful years. This approach will also shed new light on familiar themes – on his oft-repeated statement that, 'For me a film is 99 per cent finished with the screenplay', on his preferred pace of filming; on his special attraction to a varied selection of film projects, as well as on the many changes that took place when he moved to Hollywood.

For those less familiar with Hitchcock and his films, this book will provide a useful introduction to his work, at the same time presenting a new perspective on his career that should appeal to the more sophisticated student or film buff who may already be familiar with many of the films and with some of the vast amount that has already been written about him.

No director in the history of the cinema has succeeded better in balancing one film against another, in balancing hits against flops, or smaller, more intimate and personal films against larger, more commercial ventures, British subjects with American or international ones, black-and-white with colour, even studio-bound productions with films making special use of locations. He virtually never had two flops in a row, demonstrating time and again a remarkable ability to bounce back from failure with renewed vigour and new success.

This pattern, of balancing one film against another, year after year, was actually first established by Hitchcock as a natural response to the pressures of filming in Hollywood with generally larger budgets and the greater risks involved. Beginning with his first American productions he alternated very different types of projects from film to film and studio to studio, apparently able to exercise a surprisingly large degree of control over his career. At the same time he continued to make his features at a steady pace, averaging one per year up to the early 1960s, often setting himself new challenges while staying mainly within the overall suspense or thriller genre.

These three interrelated elements can perhaps be singled out as crucial to an understanding of his development in Hollywood: (1) control over the choice of films, (2) a measured pace of filming, and (3) a great variety of projects.

Although Hitchcock was initially under a long-term contract to David Selznick, when he first arrived the producer gave up making films for a number of years. Thus Hitchcock was loaned out to other producers and studios – but only for projects which he himself had selected and was keen to do. This was made easier by the fact that Hitchcock was much in demand at the time, though it is worth noting that he worked mainly for the smaller or more moderate-sized companies. Aside from the Selznick studio, there was Wanger/UA, Universal and RKO. In addition, he was able to serve more or less as his own producer and was able to maintain a large degree of creative control.

Many critics have made the point that Hitchcock was given more generous budgets and provided with greater technical resources in Hollywood than he had been used to in Britain. His first two features both cost well over $1 million, for example, two to three times larger than the budgets of his British thrillers during the late 1930s. He spent a lot of time on each project, involving himself in all aspects of the films from the initial scripting, the design, photography and overall 'look' of the film, up to the final edit. Known for his outstanding technical expertise, he was especially proud of some of the technical effects he achieved in *Foreign Correspondent*, for example. There was obviously a greater opportunity in Hollywood for a visually aware film-maker like Hitchcock.

Yet if three of his first four American productions (including *Suspicion*) were more stylish, glossy and expensive-looking than his British films, the two pictures that followed, at Universal, were more modest efforts, costing under $1 million each. With *Saboteur* he even adapted to an American wartime setting one of his most successful British plot lines, concerning an innocent man who is implicated in a crime and on the run while trying to clear himself and catch the real culprits.

With the larger resources of the American cinema available to him, Hitchcock recognized that he now had an attractive new range of choices. He thus made a number of large and moderately expensive pictures and worked with top stars, yet there were many modest films as well. Hitch's response to filming in the US appears to have been to develop a whole new pattern of film-making that would continue throughout the rest of his career. He never made two similar pictures in a row. He had not left Britain far behind, either, for he continued to make the occasional British or part-British films, either using British actors in Hollywood or returning to Britain to film from time to time.

There had been a period during the early sound years, from *Blackmail* (1929) up to *The Man Who Knew Too Much* (1934), when Hitchcock had alternated between thrillers and other types of films in a somewhat random fashion. But rather than being planned or controlled by him, this was actually dictated by his lack of choice at the time, having to take on those projects that he was offered or assigned by the studio. As he later recalled to François Truffaut,

> *Rich and Strange* had been a disappointment, and *Number 17* reflected a careless approach to my work [both released in 1932]. There was no careful analysis of what I was doing. Since those days I've learned to be very self-critical, to step back and take a second look. And never to embark on a project unless there's an inner feeling of comfort about it . . . If the basic concept is solid, things will work out. What happens to the film, of course, becomes a matter of degree, but there should be no question that the concept is a sound one.   (Truffaut)

Ten years later, Hitchcock had settled in Hollywood. He had become far more disciplined in his approach to potential film projects and undoubtedly benefited from the fact that, even though he continued to make his home in California up to his death in 1980, he never became fully Americanized. Extremely conservative in his dress and behaviour, he was set apart from most other Hollywood directors. He and his wife generally avoided the Hollywood parties and night life, though his one indulgence was a love of good food and wine. He was also a bit of a practical joker and many examples of his off-beat sense of humour can be found in his films. Not only was his Britishness reflected in his personal life and dealings with the film industry, but it also influenced his choice of film projects and his approach to directing. He was able to maintain a degree of detachment that was very important to him, since he often found it difficult to decide what picture to do next. In fact, throughout his years in Hollywood he remained surprisingly insecure regarding his choice of films, in spite of his great success there. But fortunately, his special ability to visualize the completed picture even before filming had begun meant that he was often able to recognize an unsuitable project in time to drop it. Not only did his pre-production expertise allow him to feel more secure about each individual project, but this also fitted in well with his efforts to vary his pictures as much as possible. He would generally begin work on his next production very soon after completing his previous one and thus was able to develop those new and different qualities that appealed to him most, with his just completed film still fresh in his mind.

In addition, Hitchcock accommodated himself well to the Hollywood star system. He got on well with most of the stars he cast in his films and developed a particularly close working relationship with his favourites, including Ingrid Bergman, Cary Grant, James Stewart and Grace Kelly. Unlike some directors, who did not like being forced to use leading stars, Hitchcock appreciated the fact that stars provided added insurance at the box office, especially for some of his less commercial projects. (He was actually disappointed when forced to settle for lesser actors earlier in his Hollywood career before his name was well enough known; but few stars turned him down in later years.) His interest in varying his films meant that he would often use the same actor in quite different roles. The best examples here are the three very different parts played by Ingrid Bergman in the 1940s and by James Stewart in the 1950s. Though often underrated for his qualities as a fine director of actors, Hitchcock's strong sense of what he was setting out to accomplish in each film meant that their performances were seen by him as but one important element within his total conception of the work in which the editing, photography and overall 'look' of the film could be equally important.

Yet he typically allowed his actors a great deal of freedom to develop their roles without interference from him, just as long as their performance fitted within his general scheme. As his actress daughter later recalled,

> He wanted an actor to bring something to the part, and he would not do any direction until he saw a rehearsal first and he saw what the actor would bring to it. Then he very quietly would talk to the actor, you know, and say, 'Now I think it might be . . . why don't you try such and such a thing,' and of course you did and it worked beautifully. But there were no bombastic ravings or anything like that on the set. The sets were very quiet and very happy and very normal. (Leff)

Stars such as Ingrid Bergman, James Stewart, Cary Grant and Grace Kelly loved to work with him, while others who only appeared in a single film often had pleasant memories of working with Hitchcock.

Thus, Bernard Miles recalled the filming of *The Man Who Knew Too Much* in 1955:

> He always seemed more concerned with technical matters than with the actors, and he gave us all the impression that this was a leisurely enterprise, and that he was just along for the ride. I remember James Stewart telling me, 'We're in the hands of an expert here. You can lean on him. Just do everything he tells you, and the whole thing will be okay.' I took his advice, and it was a very genial experience . . . (Spoto, *Life*)

Similarly, Ann Todd had never worked on an American production before when she was cast in *The Paradine Case* in 1946, and she quite appreciated Hitchcock's methods:

> He takes the trouble to study his actors quite apart from what they are playing and so is able to bring hidden things out from them. He always realized how nervous I was and used to wait for silence before 'Action' and then tell a naughty, sometimes shocking story that either galvanized me into action or collapsed me into giggles: either way it removed the tension. (Spoto, *Life*)

It is, however, a bit difficult to understand Hitchcock's apparent reluctance to film American subjects during his first decade in Hollywood in the 1940s, which meant that he used American stars quite sparingly. For, when he did turn to stories set in the US, as with *Shadow of a Doubt*, *Strangers on a Train* and the superb run of films during 1956–64, he often came up with the most remarkable results.

In fact, Hitchcock had been interested in America, and especially New York City, from an early age. In conversation with Truffaut he admitted that, 'later on I often wondered about the fact that I made no attempt to visit America until 1937; I'm still puzzled about that. I was meeting Americans all the time and was completely familiar with the map of New York . . . Years before I ever came here, I could describe New York, tell you where the theatres and stores were located . . .' Aside from the more familiar excuses – that he had difficulty finding the right projects or finding writers who could collaborate with him on the scripts (a very important consideration), there appears to be no obvious explanation. For it seems clear that Hitchcock was originally attracted to the US, not only for the opportunities presented by its film industry, but for all the imaginative possibilities suggested by American movie subjects – the diversity of American culture and society ('there are no Americans', he said, 'America is full of foreigners'), the drama, violence and sheer excitement of the place, and the great variety of landscapes and settings. (He preferred to film on location whenever possible.)

Hitchcock, his cast and crew spent about two weeks rehearsing before they began filming *Rope* late in January 1948. This still gives some idea of the kind of technical equipment required for shooting the film entirely within a single apartment set making use of extremely long takes. Hitch stands beside the Technicolor camera which is enclosed in its sound proof box (or blimp) and mounted on a mobile crane, while the microphones are attached to long booms overhead and a vast array of lights gaze down from above.

Hitchcock's fifth Hollywood production, *Saboteur*, was his first American thriller, for example, and he followed it with his most memorable American subject of the 1940s, *Shadow of a Doubt* (1943), partly filmed on location, in which he demonstrated a remarkable ability to capture Americans and American society on the screen in a very special and personal way. Yet it would be many years before he would repeat the experiment. His few other American subjects tended to be very studio-bound – *Mr and Mrs Smith* (1941), *Spellbound* (1945) and *Rope* (1948). These were balanced by his international productions (with multinational casts) – *Foreign Correspondent* (1940), *Lifeboat* (1944) and *Notorious* (1946) – and by his many British productions, either filmed in Hollywood – *Rebecca* (1940), *Suspicion* (1941), and *The Paradine Case* (1947) – or back in Britain *Under Capricorn* (1949) and *Stage Fright* (1950). Thus, the limited extent of his attraction to American subjects initially also reflects the pattern of diversity, a pattern that continued on into the 1950s. The few American films are generally interspersed among the other British or international features, up to *The Wrong Man* in 1956, which began the most American period of his career.

It is also worth noting that, for Hitchcock, artistic and commercial success often go together. Thus, many of his most memorable pictures – *Notorious*, *Rear Window*, *North by Northwest* and *Psycho* – were also big hits, while *Rebecca*, *Shadow of a Doubt*, *Strangers on a Train* and *The Birds* all earned reasonable profits. Only *The Wrong Man*, *Vertigo* and *Marnie* were major disappointments at the box office, and of the three, *Vertigo* at least broke even (and possibly made a small profit).

At this point, a general chronological assessment of Hitchcock's American years may help to bring together various of the themes that have been noted above, paying particular attention to the hits and flops, and providing a useful framework for the more detailed discussion of the individual films in the main chapters that follow.

Hitchcock's years as a film-maker in the US, from 1939 to 1976, can be divided into five main periods. The first period, from 1939 to 1946, begins with the Oscar-winning *Rebecca* and concludes with his two biggest hits of the 1940s – *Spellbound* and *Notorious*. The second period covers his most difficult years from 1947 to 1950, and include two major flops – *The Paradine Case* and *Under Capricorn* – and only one moderate success (*Rope*). In the third period, from 1950 to 1955, he experienced a gradual recovery at Warners that turned into major success at Paramount in 1954–5. The fourth period, from 1955 to 1960, was his most creative and most American period, mainly at Paramount, with a diverse group of remarkable films, such as *The Wrong Man* and *Vertigo*, and two of his biggest hits – *North by Northwest* and *Psycho*. The final period at Universal from 1961 to 1976 saw his career wind down. The films were fewer and farther between and generally disappointing, with one disastrous flop – *Topaz*.

1939–46

Hitchcock quickly became an important figure in Hollywood, achieving Oscar recognition and success at the box office. Demonstrating a special flair for self publicity, he turned himself into one of the best known and most readily identifiable director figures in Hollywood. Staying generally within the suspense drama or thriller genre, he made a variety of films and initially worked at a slightly faster pace, completing his first six pictures in the US in slightly under four years (1939–42). He also made good use of a diverse group of stars and technicians, adapting well to the different requirements of filming at a number of different studios. Of special importance here is the fact that he had made a really major contribution to three different studios within a short space of time – United Artists, RKO and Universal.

Under contract to UA producer David Selznick, then loaned to Walter Wanger, Hitchcock found himself in good company at United Artists during 1939–40 when the quality of its pictures from leading Hollywood directors and producers was quite remarkable. Films of note included *Stagecoach* and *The Long Voyage Home* from director John Ford and producer Wanger, *Wuthering Heights* and *The Westerner* from director William Wyler and producer Sam Goldwyn, Charlie Chaplin's last big success, *The Great Dictator*, also *Of Mice and Men* and *A Chump at Oxford* from producer Hal Roach and *The Four Feathers* and *The Thief of Baghdad* from British producer Alexander Korda. (Unfortunately, virtually all of these producers and directors would leave UA within a few years.)

Hitchcock contributed *Rebecca* – the first ever UA production to win the Best Picture Oscar – and the equally impressive, if somewhat less profitable, *Foreign Correspondent*, also nominated for the Oscar as Best Picture, as was *Spellbound* (from Hitchcock and Selznick) five years later. With UA shaky financially throughout most of the 1940s, Hitchcock and Selznick did their bit to keep the company afloat: *Rebecca* was UA's top hit of 1940, while *Spellbound* was the biggest hit of the decade.

On *Rebecca*, Hitchcock had been forced by producer Selznick to remain more faithful to the novel than he had originally intended. But having been signed by Wanger for his second American feature even before the filming of *Rebecca* had been completed, he already knew that it would be more to his taste.

Continuing to vary his projects, Hitchcock then made an American screwball comedy for RKO – very different indeed! – and followed this with a return to women's suspense fiction set in England in the *Rebecca* tradition, with Joan Fontaine once again as the star. The filming of *Mr and Mrs Smith* went smoothly and according to plan, but it was during the production of *Suspicion*, his second picture for RKO, that he was forced to deal with pressures from the executives of a large Hollywood studio for the first time.

In attempting to understand Hitchcock's position in Hollywood at this time and in the light of their later careers, it is revealing to compare his difficulties on *Suspicion* with those of Orson Welles who happened to be at the same studio, filming *The Magnificent Ambersons*, later that same year (1941). The conventional view of the two men is that Welles was a victim of the Hollywood system and was treated badly by the studio, in contrast to Hitchcock who was generally regarded as a more commercially reliable producer-director. But, in fact, the studio was equally ready to put pressure on Hitchcock as both he and Welles were faced with similar difficulties, namely a general studio hostility to the main theme of their films and a problem with their endings after running over budget. (At $1.25 million, *Suspicion* was more costly than the $1 million *Ambersons*. Problems with the script, rising costs and no end in sight owing to Hitchcock's slow pace of filming, meant that the studio had even considered scrapping the entire production at one point.)

The big difference in the result was that Hitchcock refused to be rushed or intimidated by the studio bosses. He filmed an ending that works reasonably well, and although an RKO producer apparently tried to recut the film to excise all hints that Cary Grant might be a murderer, thus eliminating all the film's tension and suspense, it was finally released in Hitchcock's version. Welles, involved in three different projects simultaneously, was in South America filming *It's All True* when unfavourable early previews of *Ambersons* caused the studio to panic. Since he was not around to defend his version, and none of his associates were influential enough to stand up to the studio in his place, a new ending was substituted and the film was drastically recut. Its release in this butchered version was disastrous. When *It's All True* was also cancelled by the new studio management, this marked the beginning of the end for Welles as a Hollywood director, forever labelled as 'difficult'. In contrast, *Suspicion* ended up as RKO's most profitable and successful movie of 1941 and contributed significantly to the revival of the company's profits in the early 1940s. Thus, Hitchcock was quickly forgiven and went on to consolidate his position as a leading Hollywood director. In spite of the fact that three of his first four pictures in the US had gone over budget and had averaged a substantial cost of $1.3 million each, two of the three had been hits, thus proving that the quality of the results, not costs, were what mattered. Hitchcock would even return to RKO five years later to provide the studio with one of its biggest hits of the 1940s – *Notorious*.

Hitchcock was next loaned out to Universal where he directed two features during 1941–2. The brief period he spent at this studio was not at all typical of his film-making during the 1940s. Yet he did demonstrate while there that he was capable of filming more economically and that he was quite willing and able to work at one of the smaller and less prestigious Hollywood studios – filming more on location, foregoing costly sets and elaborate special effects and with less expensive stars – when an opportunity presented itself that appealed to him. Here he made two films that were quite different from anything he had tried in the US before. Just as *Rebecca* was followed by an international spy thriller, after *Suspicion* Hitchcock filmed *Saboteur*, a topical espionage thriller set in the US, while the mystery murder drama *Shadow of a Doubt* that followed was notable as his most imaginative use of a small-town family setting and 40s location filming.

Universal was trying to upgrade its image in the early 1940s, having recently returned to profitability after a disastrous 30s. Not only did Hitchcock's presence add to the studio's growing prestige, but also, as with UA and RKO, he contributed significantly to the company's balance sheet. (Both productions cost under $1 million and earned good profits.)

Unfortunately, Hitchcock's last loanout, to 20th Century-Fox, was also the least successful. Here he had set himself a new and different challenge – of confining the film to the single setting of a lifeboat stranded at sea. But serious problems with the script meant that once again the filming ran far over schedule and over budget. The result was his most expensive American picture thus far. And this time, unlike his previous films, it failed to do well at the box office. Thus, *Lifeboat*, his only production for one of the top four studios, was also the worst flop of his early years in Hollywood. (Fox probably lost as much on this film as RKO had done with the much more widely publicized example of *The Magnificent Ambersons*.)

Returning to producer David Selznick in 1944, Hitchcock collaborated closely with writer Ben Hecht on two projects – a psychological thriller with a psychiatry theme and a romantic spy drama. The contrast between them provides yet another example of his ability to vary his films, even when both had the same writer-and-producer collaborators and the same star (Ingrid Bergman).

Not only had Hitchcock made a remarkable variety of pictures during 1939–46, but there was also a clear pattern of pairings that would continue throughout his American career. Two contrasting films for UA, RKO, Universal and Selznick, with only *Lifeboat* for Fox as the odd film out. (He was originally meant to make two pictures for Fox, too, but the filming of *Lifeboat* took so long that the second project was dropped.)

In addition, Hitchcock's commercial success up to 1946 (again with the exception of *Lifeboat*) reflected the general trends taking place at the US box office in the 1940s. He contributed to the revival of three different studios at a time of general recovery, while his two biggest hits, *Spellbound* and *Notorious* happened to coincide with the boom years of the decade.

1947–50

The severe postwar fall in US movie-going and box-office receipts is a well-documented phenomenon. But what is surprising is that this trend is so clearly reflected in the box-office figures for a single director such as Hitchcock. These were, in fact, the worst years of his American career and it is not difficult to see why. The box-office (rental) figures for his pictures can be recorded year by year to provide an unambiguous picture of his experience during this period, as presented in the accompanying chart. This clearly shows the decline in the late 1940s and recovery in the 50s.

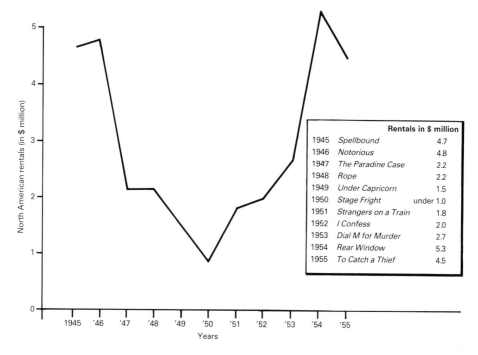

	Rentals in $ million
1945 *Spellbound*	4.7
1946 *Notorious*	4.8
1947 *The Paradine Case*	2.2
1948 *Rope*	2.2
1949 *Under Capricorn*	1.5
1950 *Stage Fright*	under 1.0
1951 *Strangers on a Train*	1.8
1952 *I Confess*	2.0
1953 *Dial M for Murder*	2.7
1954 *Rear Window*	5.3
1955 *To Catch a Thief*	4.5

Although these figures provide a general guide to the profitability of Hitchcock's pictures, note that the worst losses occurred in the declining phase only, when 3 out of the 4 films (during 1947–50) were flops.

All films listed by year of release with the exception of *I Confess*, filmed in 1952, and *Dial M for Murder*, filmed in 1953, both released early the following year.

These were difficult and unusual years for Hitchcock in many respects. Most serious of all was the fact that three out of four features released during 1947–50 flopped badly at the box office. Though perhaps this is not too surprising given that these included his two most expensive productions of the 1940s: *The Paradine Case* at $4 million had run far over budget, while *Under Capricorn* was a costume picture filmed in Technicolor at a cost of $2.5 million. (If even a slight adjustment is made for inflation, it is clear that *Paradine* was by far the most expensive picture of his entire career, while second place is too close to call – a virtual tie between *Notorious, North by Northwest* and *Under Capricorn*.) But although *Rope* and *Stage Fright* had each cost substantially less, at about $1.5 million, this was not nearly low enough, given the shaky state of the box office during the post-war years. In fact, *Rope* was the only film that earned a small profit, while *Stage Fright* recorded a small loss.

An additional indication of his lack of success is the fact that his films received only one Oscar nomination in four years – for Ethel Barrymore's performance, as supporting actress, in *The Paradine Case*. Having previously contributed in important ways to the development and maturing of the American cinema in the 1940s and to various leading studios in particular, and having attained such stature and fame as one of the leading directors in Hollywood, Hitchcock, surprisingly, seems to have distanced himself from the American film industry during these years.

Admittedly, this was not entirely his own decision. For example, producer David Selznick had left United Artists by the time of *The Paradine Case* in 1946–7, their last film together, having decided to distribute his pictures himself. Hitchcock set up his own 'Anglo-American' production company, called, appropriately, Transatlantic Pictures, formed in partnership with British producer Sidney Bernstein. There was a strong hint here that Hitchcock would be dividing his time between Hollywood and London (with Warner Brothers as the American distributor).

In fact, Hitchcock made only two pictures for Transatlantic – *Rope*, filmed in the US, and *Under Capricorn*, filmed in England, then remained in Britain to make *Stage Fright*, his first production under a new four-picture deal with Warner Bros. Quite clearly, this period was dominated by British themes, including his first two features filmed in England since his departure for the US in 1939 and *The Paradine Case*, a very British subject with a mainly British cast, though filmed in Hollywood. In addition, his three features during 1946–8 all made use of expensive and elaborate sets at a time when the trend in much of Hollywood filming was to go out on location (ironically, a development that Hitch himself had helped to pioneer so effectively with *Shadow of a*

Doubt a number of years earlier). This was a very studio-bound period for Hitchcock, when he experimented with new ways of studio filming. He used multiple-camera techniques to shoot some of the important courtroom sequences within the large and impressive Old Bailey set built in Hollywood for *The Paradine Case*. Then he experimented with extremely long takes in filming both *Rope*, and *Under Capricorn*. *Rope* took place entirely within a single, elaborate apartment set making use of takes which lasted from five to nine minutes each. *Under Capricorn* was a costume drama set in nineteenth century Australia and required many elaborately designed interiors. Both of these pictures were made in Technicolor at a time when the vast majority of the leading Hollywood directors were still shooting dramatic pictures in black-and-white, yet another element serving to differentiate Hitchcock during these years from the rest of Hollywood. (Throughout the 1940s the colour films made in Hollywood were predominantly musicals.)

Whereas *Rope* turned out to be a moderately interesting and modestly successful experiment, the extremely costly *Under Capricorn* suffered from a weak script and was a big lossmaker. On the whole Hitchcock's brief and rather unenterprising venture into independent production was a major disappointment. He then returned to a more modest and familiar style of black-and-white film-making with the thriller *Stage Fright*, including a fair amount of location filming in England – a first step towards the kind of black-and-white productions that would mark his comeback in the US in the early 1950s. Unfortunately, this film too suffered from a weak script and miscasting in the lead roles, and represented yet another bad choice for Hitchcock during these difficult years. Filmed at a cost of about $1.5 million, at least it was not especially expensive, which meant that it lost far less money than *Under Capricorn* or *The Paradine Case*.

1950–55

In 1950, Hitchcock returned to making the kind of American *film noir* that he could do so well and had not tried for far too many years. Filmed in black-and-white by a new, favourite cameraman, Robert Burks, making effective use of location photography, and with an ingenious story and script, *Strangers on a Train* marked a major first step for Hitchcock towards reclaiming his position as a top Hollywood director and a leading force in the American cinema.

This meant, for example, that he began to use American stars in his pictures more than ever before, resuming his congenial collaboration with James Stewart on *Rear Window* in 1953 – the first of their three films together in the 1950s – and working especially well with a new young American actress named Grace Kelly. Not surprisingly, he appears to have been more attracted to American subjects at the same time, though this would become more clearly apparent in the late 1950s. Beginning with relatively modestly budgeted black-and-white pictures, he then returned to larger budgets and colour at a time when his productions were doing better at the box office. In fact, the trend for Hitchcock, in particular, closely resembles that for the American main-stream cinema as a whole: the move into colour in 1953–5 in conjunction with the introduction of a new range of techniques including 3–D, CinemaScope, VistaVision and Cinerama, helped to boost box-office receipts and reverse the previous decline.

In addition, Hitchcock once again became more closely involved with the leading American movie studios. He made a modest contribution to Warner Bros in the early 1950s, including one film in colour and 3–D, the studio's favourite new process, first introduced in 1953 (but just as quickly dropped the following year).

He provided MGM with one of its biggest hits of the late '50s with *North by Northwest*. Of special significance was his new, highly favour-able deal with Paramount in 1953, just as the studio was losing a number of its leading directors: Frank Capra had left in 1951, followed by George Stevens early in 1953; Billy Wilder would leave in 1954 and William Wyler in 1955. Thus, it would not take Hitchcock long to establish himself as the leading Paramount director, a position that he would maintain throughout most of the period from 1954 to 1960.

Hitchcock quickly demonstrated his value to the studio during 1954–5 as his first two productions, *Rear Window* and *To Catch a Thief*, both starring Grace Kelly, turned out to be smash hits. Suddenly he was back in favour with critics and audiences, better known and more successful than ever before. Between them, these two films were nominated for seven Oscars. Hitchcock was himself nominated for directing (*Rear Window*) for the first time since *Spellbound*, nine years earlier, while *To Catch a Thief*, filmed in the studio's new VistaVision process, won the Oscar for best colour cinematography.

Having made his home in California since 1939, the slow process of Hitchcock's 'Americanization' also suddenly began to speed up in the mid-1950s. He finally took the plunge and became an American citizen in 1955, the same year that he would establish himself as a leading media figure in the· US by developing a new interest in television, too. His highly popular television series, *Alfred Hitchcock Presents*, first appeared in the autumn of 1955, and since he personally introduced all

One of Hitchcock's most entertaining, if relatively lightweight, productions of the fifties, *To Catch a Thief* was quite stunningly photographed in Paramount's new VistaVision process in 1954 and won an Oscar for cinematography for Robert Burks, Hitch's favourite cameraman. [It was the first of the director's five VistaVision films, qualifying him as the most important director to work with this relatively shortlived, but excellent, camera system.]

the episodes himself, his face became more familiar to audiences than ever before. There was even a successful venture into publishing with *Alfred Hitchcock's Mystery Magazine* and his name appeared on various anthologies of suspense and crime stories 'edited by Alfred Hitchcock'. Clearly, Hitchcock's recovery from the difficult years of the late 1940s was complete.

1955–60

This period clearly represents the culmination of Hitchcock's development as a director in Hollywood. Having experienced success in the 1940s, followed by a period of decline and then recovery in the 1950s, he now felt more confident and secure about his position at Paramount. Here he assembled an outstanding team of collaborators who would remain with him for many years, and, added to the success of his television series, three out of his first four Paramount productions were big hits. From 1953 on, he was working continuously in colour for the first time and using the excellent VistaVision cameras during 1955–9. Filming extensively on location, he divided his interest between the East Coast (*The Trouble with Harry* and *The Wrong Man*, followed by *Marnie* in 1963) and the West Coast (*Vertigo*, *Psycho* and *The Birds*) and crossed the country from New York to South Dakota in *North by Northwest*.

Throughout the 1950s, Hitchcock kept up his one film per year average in spite of his other activities. He continued to make a variety of pictures, balancing one against another so that they actually form a natural series of contrasting pairs, much as he had done for the different companies in the 1940s. The personal projects such as *I Confess*, *Rear Window* and *The Trouble with Harry* were each followed by a more 'commercial' and expensive venture – *Dial M for Murder* (in 3–D and colour), *To Catch a Thief* and *The Man Who Knew Too Much* (both making use of colourful international settings filmed in VistaVision). But from 1956 on he felt confident enough to give up making the more obviously commercial or conventional films, beginning quite appropriately with *The Wrong Man*, one of his most unusual and remarkable films. Yet he continued to vary his projects so that the more difficult and unusual subjects, such as *The Wrong Man* and *Psycho*, were filmed more quickly and cheaply (in black-and-white), 'paired' respectively with *Vertigo* and *North by Northwest* (in colour and VistaVision).

Hitchcock directs Janet Leigh in one of the most famous sequences ever, the shower murder scene in *Psycho*. Visual consultant Saul Bass provided an elaborate storyboard for filming, while the piercing strings sound, devised by composer Bernard Herrmann, once heard can never be forgotten. [The scene was often imitated by later film-makers, but none of them could match the impact of Hitchcock's first, audacious venture into horror.]

During these years of unparalleled success and activity in films and television, in his late fifties, when one might expect him to show signs of being overstretched and perhaps a bit neglectful of his film career, his judgment (in selecting projects) and skills as a director are clearly demonstrated in one outstanding film after another. For example, he successfully resisted the all too obvious temptation to try and make each succeeding film bigger and grander than the preceding one – especially in contrast to the 25-minute black-and-white thriller sketches of his television show. But having worked regularly in colour and VistaVision, he happily returned to black-and-white filming when the subject warranted. This is most clearly seen in the last pairing of the decade and the contrast between *North by Northwest*, $2\frac{1}{4}$ hours long with a starry cast and a cost of \$4.3 million, and the black-and-white *Psycho*, filmed quickly and cheaply on a budget of less than \$1 million. But, ironically, it was this latter, his last picture for Paramount, that turned out to be the biggest hit and most profitable film of his entire career, also earning him the last of his five Oscar nominations for directing. Yet it was his blackest and most scary film, reflecting on the darker side of human behaviour.

In alternating between colour and black-and-white in the late 1950s, Hitchcock was following the general trend in the American cinema when many leading directors returned to black-and-white. But Hitchcock's name, during his Paramount years, must be for ever linked with the studio's high quality widescreen process – VistaVision. No other director made so many remarkable and successful VistaVision films during the relatively brief life of the process, concentrated mainly into the years 1955–9. Hitchcock directed one of the first big VistaVision hits, the Oscar-winning *To Catch a Thief*, in 1955, and the very last big success in 1959 with *North by Northwest* – he specially took the cameras with him to MGM for this one, clearly proving that he appreciated the quality of the VistaVision system. Most interesting of all, he demonstrated the creative possibilities of VistaVision in filming *Vertigo*, his fourth picture using this process and one of his most remarkable achievements.

However, it was the extraordinary *Psycho* that brought this, the most outstanding period of Hitchcock's career, to an end in 1960.

1961–76

When Hitchcock's agents, the giant MCA headed by Lew Wasserman, took over the Universal Studios in the early 1960s, it was natural for him to move from Paramount to Universal, where he had already been making his television series. Here he would set up his offices and produce his last six features. There were other changes, too. Having passed his sixtieth birthday, he now worked at a slower pace, averaging one film every two years, then with gaps of three and finally four years between productions. And he began to work with a new and generally younger generation of stars, a trend that was first evident in *Psycho*. But after the tremendous successes of the 1950s, a decline was inevitable.

Still attracted to American subjects and settings, he relocated Daphne du Maurier's story 'The Birds' from Cornwall to Northern California. *Marnie* (1963–4) was his last East Coast movie, a superb psychological crime drama that was not fully appreciated by audiences or critics at the time it was first released.

If *Torn Curtain*, which followed, was a not entirely successful return to the international spy thriller genre, with Paul Newman and Julie Andrews uneasily cast in the leading roles, *Topaz* (1969) was perhaps the worst disaster of Hitchcock's years in Hollywood, with little to recommend it to even the most avid Hitchcock fans. But in Hitchcock's defence it should be pointed out that the 1969–70 years were disastrous at the box office for most of the top Hollywood studios, and Hitchcock was but one of the many distinguished directors who were in serious difficulties at this time. (For example, John Huston was at the low point of his career with *Sinful Davey* and *A Walk with Love and Death*, both released in 1969, and Billy Wilder had his biggest ever flop with *The Private Life of Sherlock Holmes* (1970), while the directing careers of George Stevens (*The Only Game in Town*), William Wyler (*The Liberation of L.B. Jones*) and Howard Hawks (*Rio Lobo*) came to a disappointing end in 1970.)

Fortunately, after the failure of *Topaz*, Hitchcock returned to form in the 1970s with his last two features. He neatly rounded off his career with one last visit to England to shoot *Frenzy* in 1971 and filmed *Family Plot* back in California in 1975. Both were moderately successful and were treated respectfully by audiences and critics alike, but the characteristically Hitchcockian touches appeared a bit laboured and old fashioned and neither film really came alive on the screen.

Over ten years after Hitchcock's death and almost twenty years since his last film, his cinematic legacy looks as strong as ever. Many of his best pictures have been re-released to cinemas and are seen regularly on television and on video. But most of all, he succeeded so well in putting his personal stamp on two of the most popular genres of the cinema, the suspense thriller and the horror movie (with *Psycho* in particular), that his influence is readily apparent in a large number of pictures being made today, and will probably continue to be so as long as films continue to be made.

2

1939-40:
Hitchcock and Selznick

Rebecca and *Foreign Correspondent*

Hitchcock had become interested in America and the American cinema from an early age. He first began reading the film trade papers at the age of 16 and was first attracted to working for an American, rather than a British, film company, a few years later. 'In actual fact, I started out in 1921 in an American film studio that happened to be located in London [Famous Players-Lasky in Islington] and never set foot in a British studio until 1927.'

Hitch was first employed in the titles department in 1920, but since it was a small studio, he was able to familiarize himself with every aspect of the film-making process. He graduated to head of the editorial department, did some script writing, served as an assistant director and editor and had even designed sets and costumes before he was given the opportunity to direct his first feature, *The Pleasure Garden*, in 1925. Though he directed a variety of pictures during these early years, Hitch had his biggest success with thrillers such as *The Lodger* (1926) and *Blackmail* (1929). By the mid-1930s, when he emerged as the leading British film-maker, he had become most clearly associated with the suspense and thriller genre, with such outstanding successes as *The Man Who Knew Too Much* (1934) and *The 39 Steps* (1935), as well as *Secret Agent* and *Sabotage* (both released in 1936). But he never felt that he was really appreciated in Britain and was well aware of the British intellectual snobbery with regard to the cinema in general and the popular thrillers with which he was most closely identified in particular.

By 1937, he was becoming increasingly unhappy with filming in England on relatively modest budgets with limited technical resources. He was well aware of the opportunities offered by the large American studios. But, having enjoyed a large degree of creative freedom on his British productions, he was wary of the Hollywood studio system where

Hitchcock, script in hand, enjoys the company of three of his young actresses during a break in filming the opening scenes of *The Lady Vanishes* in 1937. (Left to right): Sally Stewart, Margaret Lockwood, the film's star, Hitchcock and Googie Withers. [The picture turned out to be his most successful of the 1930s and he won the New York Film Critics award as the outstanding director of 1938 for his work on this film.]

the contract directors generally had little control over the projects to which they were assigned. A number of Hollywood studios had expressed an interest in hiring him, and he finally visited the US for the first time in the summer of 1937 after completing the filming of his latest feature, *Young and Innocent*. The best offer he received was from independent producer David Selznick. He signed with Selznick in July 1938, shortly after completing the film that would prove to be the most popular and successful of all his British pictures, *The Lady Vanishes*, starring Michael Redgrave, Margaret Lockwood and Dame May Whitty, which earned him the New York Film Critics award as the outstanding director of the year.

Selznick was a product of the American studio system. Though almost three years younger than Hitchcock, he had first become involved in the cinema, working as an assistant in his father Lewis Selznick's film company in the early 1920s at the very same time that Hitch was employed at the Islington Studios in London. Selznick first began to make a name for himself at MGM and then as a producer at Paramount (Famous Players-Lasky) in the late 1920s at the same time that Hitch was establishing himself as a leading British director. However, it was during the early 1930s that Selznick clearly emerged as one of the most brilliant young producers in Hollywood, first as production chief at the new RKO studio, then at MGM before he left to establish his own production company, releasing his pictures through United Artists.

During the following years he further demonstrated his abilities as a producer of quality pictures with a mixture of modern dramatic subjects (*A Star is Born, Made for Each Other*) and comedies (*Nothing Sacred, Young in Heart*), but was best known for his adaptations of classic novels, such as *Little Lord Fauntleroy, The Prisoner of Zenda* and *Tom Sawyer.* Typically involved in every aspect of each of his films, while running his own company, Selznick soon found that, even for a workoholic like himself, this was proving to be an impossible task. As he wrote in April 1937, less than two years after he had gone independent, 'I'd like to attempt to lighten the burden by trying a combination associate producer and director position for such few men as might be capable of handling such dual responsibilities . . . Ninety-nine directors out of a hundred are worthless as producers, particularly for themselves . . .'

He was especially interested in hiring Frank Capra, who was in dispute with Columbia at this time, but Selznick also put out feelers to other leading directors including Leo McCarey, Gregory La Cava and Mervyn LeRoy as well as Hitchcock in England. But he was characteristically dismissive of the talents of George Cukor, whom he did sign up for a time, and John Ford, whom he didn't. (Ford ended up taking his current project, 'The Stage to Lordsburg', to rival UA producer Walter Wanger instead, and it became the highly successful *Stagecoach.*) 'I feel that we must dismiss Ford as a man who is no more sure-fire than is Cukor,' wrote Selznick in June 1937. 'Both are great directors and both have to have their stories selected for them and guided for them . . .'

In fact, Selznick's reputation for keeping tight control over each of his productions meant that many of the leading directors were wary of signing with him. Those who did tended to be solid craftsmen types or 'actors/directors', such as John Cromwell, William Wellman, Norman Taurog and Richard Wallace, rather than the top creative talents. Hitchcock, however, clearly fulfilled the Selznick requirements: 'What makes

Hitchcock so important is that he is a producer as well as a director actually.' Selznick probably felt that he could better control a British director, newly arrived in the US and grateful for the opportunity to work in Hollywood, than an already established American. Clearly, there was a contradiction here between his wish to hire the best producer-directors, yet retain creative control over the films himself, one that he himself was well aware of. 'I have increasingly supervised every detail [of my films], and I am aware that there have been complaints from directors on this score,' he wrote in January 1940. 'But this happens to be my production method, and if directors resent this, they don't have to work with me.'

With their very different temperaments and approaches to film-making, a clash between Selznick and Hitchcock was inevitable. Hitch was an individualistic and tough-minded director with a clear vision of each film even before he began to shoot; he would film exactly as he saw it, allowing little scope for later changes or alterations. Selznick, on the other hand, was far more insecure and unpredictable, while concerned with quality he was still commercially minded. He loved to tinker with the completed footage, trying different ways of re-editing and changing things around to get the best result. He would often recall members of the cast to reshoot sequences or add new ones after shooting was completed in spite of the great cost.

A very visual director and consummate technician, Hitch thought and worked in terms of creating a work of cinema, while Selznick was more literary in his approach to characters and dialogue and took particular pride in the faithfulness with which he adapted many novels for the screen. As Hitchcock explained it: 'There are two schools of thought there. One producer I worked for insisted that a novel be followed meticulously, especially if it was a bestseller, because then the public, having read the scene, would want to see it come to life on the screen . . . But my instincts are to go from the first with the visual . . . Follow the story line if you like, but retell it in cinematic form . . .'

Originally, it had been agreed by them in 1938 that Hitchcock's first American picture would be based on an original film treatment of the sinking of the *Titanic*. But Hitch himself was more enthusiastic about a recently published novel, *Rebecca* by Daphne du Maurier. Selznick had purchased the rights for the then substantial sum of $50,000 shortly after he had signed Hitch, and it was agreed to switch to this work instead.

Hitchcock then collaborated closely with his wife, Alma, regular script assistant Joan Harrison and writer Michael Hogan on an initial treatment of the book during the winter of 1938–9 after completing his last British film, *Jamaica Inn*, based on an earlier du Maurier novel. Hitchcock and his family arrived in California in April 1939, but Selznick did not see the completed treatment until early June and apparently only realised for the first time how Hitchcock planned to adapt the novel for the screen. This sparked off one of his famous, long memos, which began: 'It is my unfortunate and distressing task to tell you that I am shocked and disappointed beyond words by the treatment of *Rebecca*. I regard it as a distorted and vulgarized version of a provenly successful work . . . We bought *Rebecca* and we intend to make *Rebecca* . . .' Hitch, Harrison and the writer, Philip MacDonald, immediately set to work on a new script taking account of Selznick's criticisms and adhering more closely to the novel, while Selznick began casting the film. In fact, the producer's involvement with the production during the summer and autumn of 1939 was limited by the fact that he was devoting all his energies to completing the most expensive and ambitious movie of his career, *Gone with the Wind*.

Selznick's development of this project had actually overshadowed his relationship with Hitchcock from the very start. Having purchased the rights to the novel in 1936, he had hired Sidney Howard to write the script in 1937, around the time that he had first begun negotiations to bring Hitchcock to Hollywood. He had signed Clark Gable for the role of Rhett Butler in August 1938, just six weeks after Hitchcock had signed with him. Selznick's preoccupation with *Gone with the Wind* meant that all his plans for the future development of his company, the hiring of additional directors and the production of other films were pushed increasingly into the background.

Rebecca tells the story of the shy, young and inexperienced girl who marries the aristocratic and handsome Maxim de Winter after a brief courtship in Monte Carlo. But when she returns with him to his spectacular family mansion, Manderley, in Cornwall, she finds that he is still troubled by memories of his first wife (Rebecca), while she is intimidated by the domineering presence of his housekeeper, Mrs Danvers.

Selznick's first choice for Maxim was Ronald Colman, who turned down the role. Leslie Howard and William Powell were both considered, but finally Selznick and Hitchcock agreed on Laurence Olivier, who had recently experienced his first big American success as the star of *Wuthering Heights* for producer Sam Goldwyn. The well known stage actress Judith Anderson was selected for Mrs Danvers, though she had only appeared on the screen once before, in the crime drama *Blood Money* in 1933. But the big problem was the casting of the insecure young heroine. With a reputation as a producer of having 'discovered' a number of leading Hollywood actresses, beginning with Katharine Hepburn (at RKO) in the early 1930s, Selznick was hoping to complete a memorable triple in 1939 following Vivien Leigh (in *Gone with the Wind*) and Ingrid Bergman, his new Swedish discovery who was just completing her first American film *Intermezzo*.

The lead role in *Rebecca* presented the ideal opportunity for launching yet another new young star. So, not surprisingly, Selznick decided to publicize his search for an actress much as he had done with Scarlett O'Hara. Hitchcock, however, 'found it a little embarrassing testing women who I knew in advance were unsuitable'. Olivier was naturally eager that the role should go to his prospective wife in real life, Vivien Leigh, but she was never a serious candidate. The final choice was between two young actresses – Anne Baxter, who had never acted on the screen before, and the partly British Joan Fontaine, who had appeared in a number of pictures mainly as a contract star at RKO in the late 1930s.

A warm and touching moment of reconciliation near the end of *Rebecca* when the young wife (Joan Fontaine) embraces her unhappy husband (Laurence Olivier) having at last learned the truth about his troubled first marriage to the beautiful, but cold and domineering Rebecca. [Uncertain about their future, he exclaims, 'I've loved you my darling, but I've known all along that Rebecca would win in the end'.]

However, most of her previous roles had been small enough that it would still be possible to promote her as another Selznick 'discovery', while her film experience made it likely that she would be better able to cope with the pressures of such a large and demanding part.

Fontaine was selected only a few weeks before filming was due to begin and soon found herself working long hours under great pressure. Hitchcock provided support and encouragement and did all he could to make things easier for her, especially during the first weeks of filming. At least the insecurity that she felt fitted the shy and introverted character she was playing, provided this could be captured on the screen.

Hitch felt quite at home on the set, filming a British novel with a largely British cast, most of whom had been recruited from the large colony of British actors in Hollywood. But unfortunately, the special attention required by Fontaine and Hitch's own measured pace of filming meant that the production soon fell behind the tightly planned shooting schedule.

Since Selznick was fully occupied with post-production on *Gone with the Wind* at this time, he had left Hitchcock alone on *Rebecca*. But overworked and out of touch with the production, he became increasingly concerned at Hitchcock's slow pace and was so unhappy with the rushes that he considered cancelling the film after only a few weeks of shooting. Only the timely intervention of his wife, Irene Mayer Selznick, on whom he often depended for a more balanced view, convinced him to change his mind.

In later interviews, Hitchcock has generally been a bit disparaging in his view of *Rebecca*: 'It's a novelette really. The story is old-fashioned. There was a whole school of feminine literature at the period . . .' But the book had been a tremendously popular best-seller, it offered a ready-made audience and was, undoubtedly, a superior example of the genre. Reworking many of the themes most often associated with the nineteenth century Gothic romance, the novel is fairly successful in its evocation of the vast and mysterious mansion and the Cornish landscape where most of the story is set, combining a modern psychological realism with a sophisticated version of the Cinderella story. (The similarity to *Jane Eyre*, for example, was made even more apparent when Joan Fontaine was cast in the Hollywood movie version of that novel a few years later.)

After getting over the initial shock of seeing his first treatment rejected by Selznick, Hitch found that he was still able to draw on many of his own special qualities as a film-maker in adapting a subject that was really rather promising. The story lent itself well to filming with its concentration on three main characters within the isolated mansion setting. In addition to his proven ability to create mood and suspense on the screen, Hitchcock further developed the subjective viewpoint of the heroine, effectively making use of reaction shots of her, and shots from her point of view, to maintain the film audience's sense of identifying with her. Similarly, in his treatment of the formidable Mrs Danvers, with her mask-like face and sinister presence, Hitchcock resorted to a neat cinematic trick: she is rarely seen arriving, but appears quite suddenly and unexpectedly in shot, often startling the heroine (and us). In this way, Hitchcock also managed to introduce some characteristically sly humour into the picture not only in the opening reels, but also rather more cruelly in his treatment of the gauche heroine in Manderley. (Truffaut even suggests that Hitchcock and the writers had some fun at her expense: 'Now, this is the scene of the meal. Shall we have her drop her fork or will she upset her glass?')

Art director Lyle Wheeler's production design shows the ruins of Manderley, gutted by fire as it appears at the beginning of *Rebecca* (1940), while the famous opening words of the novel are first heard on the soundtrack: 'Last night I dreamt I went to Manderley again . . .' Hitchcock's first American production under contract to producer David O. Selznick, it won the Oscar as the Best Picture of the year.

Shooting virtually the entire film in Hollywood presented Hitchcock with a few technical challenges, and he eagerly took advantage of the resources available to him. He worked closely with the excellent production team headed by veteran cameraman George Barnes and Selznick's leading art director, Lyle Wheeler, who was shortly to win his first Oscar for his work on *Gone with the Wind*. The art department built two miniatures in the studio to represent du Maurier's imaginary Manderley and put a lot of effort into the design and construction of the interior sets. The house itself was one of the leading characters in the drama and it was essential that it was brought convincingly to life on the screen. In addition, it was important to convey the strangeness and sense of isolation of the house (to the newly-arrived young bride), located some distance from the nearest town and approached by a long driveway through thick woods (as described in the opening pages of the novel).

Hitchcock completed the main shooting of the film by the end of November, a few weeks before the lavish Atlanta premiere of *Gone with the Wind*. Now, for the first time since filming began, Selznick was free to devote himself fully to *Rebecca*. A first rough cut of the picture ran for $2\frac{1}{2}$ hours and was given a sneak preview at the end of December. During the following month Selznick supervised some re-editing and re-recording of bits of dialogue. There were a few retakes as well, including some new footage for the climatic fire at the end, a spectacular sequence that is only hinted at in the book.

The film was finally premiered at the end of March, running two hours and ten minutes, and it proved to be a tremendous success with movie audiences and critics alike. The opening credits announce 'The Selznick Studio presents its production of Daphne du Maurier's *Rebecca*', Hitchcock received only the standard credit as director. He himself regards the film as more Selznick than Hitchcock, yet it was an ideal film to launch his Hollywood career. It clearly demonstrated his qualities as a director. Impressive visually, as one might expect, the slightly unreal atmosphere of Manderley has been captured on the screen, the haunting presence of the dead Rebecca is felt, and the mood is sustained throughout with a sparing use of dialogue and background music. The performances too are quite excellent. In short, it is a veritable model of the well-made Hollywood film in virtually every respect. It is not surprising then, that Hitch was eager to involve himself in a new project that he could regard as more his own.

Early on in the shooting of *Rebecca*, Selznick had negotiated a deal with fellow UA producer Walter Wanger to loan him the services of Hitchcock for his next production, loosely based on *Personal History*, the memoirs of foreign correspondent Vincent Sheean. The main impetus for this film had been provided by the war in Europe, which had begun in the first week of September, the very week that Hitch had begun shooting *Rebecca*. Yet the subject of *Rebecca* was such that not a hint of world events was allowed to intrude. In contrast to the insular and isolated world of Rebecca and Manderley, concentrating on a small group of characters within one main setting, Hitch was attracted to the idea of a topical international thriller with a large variety of characters and settings, recalling the best of his British spy thrillers such as *The 39 Steps* and *The Lady Vanishes*. Whereas Selznick attempted to control all aspects of his productions and had forced Hitchcock to remain faithful to du Maurier, Wanger generally allowed his directors much more leeway. Hitchcock would be virtually serving as his own producer on a film which, though it drew its inspiration from the Sheean book, would be virtually a film original created for the screen. Thus, in many respects *Foreign Correspondent* (as the new film was called), with its American stars and American viewpoint, was very different from the very British *Rebecca*. It reflected Hitchcock's own wish to avoid repeating himself and his love of new and different challenges.

Wanger had experienced some trouble in raising the necessary finance after acquiring the rights to Sheean's book, while the writers he employed were unable to produce a viable script, before Hitchcock had become involved. Ready and eager to start filming as soon as possible, but aware of the inadequacies of the existing scripts, Hitchcock brought in two of his own favourite writers, Joan Harrison and Charles Bennett, who had worked on all his British thrillers in the mid-1930s.

They had a shooting script ready by the beginning of March 1940, while Hitch assembled an outstanding technical team headed by the distinguished Polish-born cameraman Rudolph Maté, production designer William Cameron Menzies, who had just won an Oscar for his work on *Gone with the Wind*, and the Russian-born art director Alexander Golitzen. They were immediately put to work designing the large number and variety of sets that were required. These included a huge city square in Amsterdam, an elaborate three-tiered set representing the interior of a windmill with huge, interlocking wheels and narrow staircases, and both exterior and interior of the aircraft that would be used to stage the stunning crash near the end of the picture. Hitchcock was especially proud of this latter sequence, and ingeniously created the desired effect by making use of back projection footage of a real plane diving toward the ocean. The camera was positioned inside the studio cockpit, behind the two pilots, and as the plane appeared about to hit the water, 5,000 gallons of water were suddenly released from two tanks. When this volume of water broke through the front of the cockpit and poured over the two men, it gave the illusion of the plane crashing into the ocean. All this was done in a single shot, without a cut. This was immediately followed by another remarkable scene showing the few survivors clinging to the wing of the downed aircraft.

Over the two hours running time, Hitchcock developed a lively mixture of action, romance, suspense and drama, flavoured by his offbeat sense of humour and all set off against the background of Europe on the brink of war. The film tells the story of a likeable but naive young American newspaper correspondent, played by Joel McCrea, who is sent abroad to cover the events taking place in Europe in August 1939. We, the movie audience, identify with him as he becomes increasingly involved in the events he is meant to be reporting and uncovers an espionage ring using an international peace organization as its cover.

In fact, the picture begins conventionally as we are introduced to the various characters in the drama, first in New York and then in London, including the attractive heroine (Laraine Day) and her father (Herbert Marshall) who is the head of the 'Universal Peace Party'. Half an hour into the film we are suddenly jolted by the shock of the assassination of the supposed Dutch statesman Van Meer (Albert Basserman) by a photographer with a gun concealed inside his camera. Hitch's staging of this sequence is another highlight of the film. The killing, which takes place in torrential rain, and the subsequent chase through a vast sea of umbrellas are visually striking. McCrea's pursuit of the assassin leads to a mysterious windmill being used by the plotters. He soon finds that he too has become implicated – a familiar example of the Hitchcock method. We identify with the hero as 'innocent bystander' who suddenly finds himself on the run and in serious trouble, trying to clear himself and convince his girlfriend of his innocence, while uncovering the network of foreign agents operating in London.

Though the main story of the film was only loosely related to the real European situation in 1939, Wanger urged Hitch to provide a topical, anti-Nazi epilogue. Ben Hecht was hired to write a new ending and the cast were hastily reassembled, a month after the main filming had been completed. There is a leap in time to the summer of 1940, exactly when the new footage was being shot, as McCrea makes an impassioned plea to America to support the British cause as the sound of bombs dropping on London can be heard outside the radio broadcasting studio. This strongly pro-British sequence, though obviously tacked on to the rest of the film, delivered an important and effective propaganda message at the time and was remarkably prescient, for the Battle of Britain was being fought just as the picture was released, less than eight weeks after the last scene was shot and over a year before America would enter the war.

A dramatic moment in *Foreign Correspondent* (1940) just prior to the out-break of war in Europe in the summer of 1939. An assassin (left) takes aim at the Dutch statesman (Albert Basserman) with a gun concealed inside his camera, while American journalist (Joel McCrea), (centre) looks innocently on. With its fictional but topical treatment of world events, the picture represented an extremely audacious and effective piece of pro-British propaganda, released in 1940, over a year before the US entered the war.

The film represented an impressive addition to the Hitchcock *oeuvre*, yet it had some obvious weaknesses – an episodic structure that doesn't hang together too well, some old-fashioned mixing of studio and location filming and a strangely dated treatment of London. But in spite of this, it was generally regarded as one of the outstanding pictures of the year and was nominated for the Academy Award as Best Picture, along with *Rebecca* and eight other films of 1940, including *The Grapes of Wrath* directed by John Ford (for 20th Century-Fox), *The Letter* directed by William Wyler (for Warner Bros), *The Philadelphia Story* (MGM) and three other films from United Artists – Chaplin's *The Great Dictator*, *Our Town*, from the Thornton Wilder play, and *The Long Voyage Home* directed by John Ford and produced by Wanger.

It was quite an achievement for Hitch to have his first American films both nominated, with *Rebecca* as the eventual winner of the Best Picture award. Between them, the two films received seventeen nominations and one or the other was included in virtually every feature film category – all four acting categories, original screenplay (*Foreign Correspondent*), adapted screenplay, (*Rebecca*, which was also nominated for editing and score), and both films were nominated for black-and-white cinematography, art direction and special effects. Such a wide range of nominations drew attention to Hitchcock's qualities as an all-round filmmaker, not only providing recognition of technical excellence but of his less well known talent as a director of actors.

Hitchcock's success at the 1940 Oscars ceremony – though he didn't win the directing award, which went to John Ford for *The Grapes of Wrath* – clearly demonstrates how quickly he had established himself in Hollywood. It is difficult to think of another foreign director who achieved such success with his first American pictures. In addition, there were important changes taking place in Hollywood at this time, particularly with regard to the position of the leading directors within the Hollywood system. Hitchcock had arrived at just the right time to play an important role himself. He would benefit from these changes in the 1940s, while his new prestige and success was such that he would also be able to contribute to the further development of a new, more independent position for directors within the system.

In fact, Hitch's reputation had been growing ever since he first arrived in the US in 1939 and began work on *Rebecca*. At the same time that he was applying himself with typical dedication to the preparation of his first feature, he had demonstrated his special talent for self publicity. He made a special effort to maintain a good relationship with the press, always ready and willing to give witty interviews and pose for photographs. And he had quickly become one of the most recognizable of directors for the public at large. For him there was no contradiction between his serious work as a film-maker and his more public image, the readily identifiable cherubic face and portly figure – given futher exposure through his trademark cameo appearances in his own films. Of special interest is the article on him that appeared in *Life* magazine in November 1939. He was featured on 'Your Hollywood Parade' on the radio a few months later, and by 1941 he already rated a jokey reference in the Preston Sturges movie about Hollywood, *Sullivan's Travels*. In addition, he benefited from the highly developed publicity machinery of the Selznick studio. Selznick even made the point himself in a letter to Frank Capra early in 1940 when he asked 'whether any studio . . . has ever given the publicity build up to a director that I have given to Alfred Hitchcock'.

1939 is widely recognised as the peak year of the Hollywood studio system – the year of *Gone with the Wind, Wuthering Heights, The Hunchback of Notre Dame, Ninotchka, Mr Smith Goes to Washington, Stagecoach, Gunga Din, Only Angels Have Wings, Young Mr Lincoln* and many more. Yet it is perhaps ironical that this system was then in the process of undergoing basic changes. The monopolistic practices of the leading companies were being challenged by the government and there soon would be important modifications to the contract system; the loss of foreign markets, wartime restrictions and the departure of key personnel to the armed services all led to a reduction in the numbers of films being produced. And there would be changes, too, in the relationship between the directors and the producers, or production companies, that employed them. This would not only be reflected in the position of the top established directors, but also in the large group of important newcomers, of which Hitchcock was a prominent example.

Ten years after the changeover to sound, which had strengthened the studio system and led to greater studio control over filming, there were signs that the top directors were beginning to regain the kind of power and creative control that they had last enjoyed during the silent era when many directors had effectively functioned as producer-directors. It was becoming increasingly apparent that the studios recognized the value of successful directors and were prepared to compete for their services if necessary. Thus, following shortly after Mervyn LeRoy's move from Warner Bros to MGM in 1938, Frank Capra left Columbia to form his own company and chose an extremely favourable production and distribution deal with Warners as the best of many possible offers; similarly, George Stevens left RKO when he was able to negotiate a better deal with Columbia, and Lubitsch switched from Paramount to MGM – all in 1939. The position of the established directors was further strengthened by the arrival of men who had already made their name in the theatre or directing abroad or in other areas of film-making, especially scriptwriting, and therefore demanded to be treated better than the typical contract director of the 1930s, who was expected to accept regular studio assignments. Perhaps the most famous example of all was the unique contract that RKO offered to Orson Welles and his Mercury Theatre Company in August 1939. Soon after this, scriptwriter Preston Sturges convinced Paramount to give him his first opportunity to direct a feature film from one of his own scripts.

These three men represented the advance guard of the new generation of directors that would include (1) new arrivals from abroad, (2) newcomers from the theatre, and (3) new directors promoted from within the film industry (see accompanying table).

Leading new directors in Hollywood, 1939–44

	Studio and year of first feature film
New arrivals from abroad	
Alfred Hitchcock (British)	Selznick/UA, 1939–40
René Clair (French)	Universal, 1940–1
Jean Renoir (French)	20th Century-Fox, 1941
Robert Siodmak (German)	Paramount, 1941
Douglas Sirk (Danish/German)	PRC/MGM, 1942
New directors from within the film industry	
Preston Sturges (writer)	Paramount, 1939–40
John Huston (writer)	Warner Bros, 1941
Fred Zinnemann (shorts director)	MGM, 1941–2
Billy Wilder (writer)	Paramount, 1942
Robert Wise (editor)	RKO, 1943–4
New arrivals from the theatre	
Orson Welles	RKO, 1940–1
Anthony Mann	Paramount, 1942
Vincente Minnelli	MGM, 1942–3
Elia Kazan	20th Century-Fox, 1944

As the table shows, for those newcomers, as with the established directors, new opportunities were available at the leading studios, and this meant that the independent producers and their main distribution company, United Artists, tended to suffer accordingly during the 1940s. The 1939–40 years represented a high point for UA and its leading producers, unmatched in the early history of the company.

UA had three films nominated for Best Picture in 1939 and five films in 1940, including its first ever winner (*Rebecca*). But in the 1940s the departure of UA's leading producers was due, at least in part, to the fact that the top directors on whom they had depended (John Ford for Wanger, William Wyler for Goldwyn, and Hitchcock, who later on refused to sign a new contract with Selznick) would all set up their own independent production companies after the war.

Hitchcock's relationship to Selznick can be seen to symbolize the kind of changes that were taking place in Hollywood around this time and even echoed the plot of one of Selznick's best known pictures, *A Star is Born*. When Hitch arrived in the US in 1939 Selznick was the big star producer who introduced him to Hollywood and helped to promote his career as a director. But by the time they separated, eight years later, Hitchcock was the famous director who would become even more successful in the 1950s, while Selznick was virtually finished as a Hollywood producer. Their relationship will be discussed at greater length in Chapter IV on the 1943–7 years, the most important period of their collaboration when they worked on three films together.

3

1940-42:
RKO and Universal

From *Mr and Mrs Smith* to *Shadow of a Doubt*

The 1940 Oscars had highlighted the start of Hitchcock's American career, yet by the time the awards ceremony had taken place, in February 1941, he had already completed the first of two films for RKO and was midway through production on the second. As the one major studio other than United Artists that regularly made deals with outside producers, RKO had been the obvious next choice of David Selznick for loaning out Hitchcock's services in 1940.

Mr and Mrs Smith, Hitchcock's third American film, represented an unusual departure for him in various respects – a familiar example of the screwball comedies of the period, from a script already written by Norman Krasna, and a project that was the closest to a conventional studio assignment of any of Hitchcock's American films. In later interviews he always insisted that he took on this picture as a favour to his friend, Carole Lombard. But writer Donald Spoto claims that a note he uncovered in the RKO archives 'tells a different story'. 'I want to direct a typical American comedy about typical Americans,' Hitchcock is alleged to have said at the time – a typically tongue-in-cheek comment, for the leading characters in *Mr and Mrs Smith* could hardly be regarded as 'typical Americans'. With its American cast and New York setting, the picture qualifies as Hitch's first really American feature, though lighting cameraman Harry Stradling and art director L.P. Williams were both British-born. (Both had worked in England in the late 1930s and arrived in the US in 1939.)

Foreign directors in Hollywood tended to be typecast, just as much as the actors, and would often find themselves assigned to pictures set in their former home countries. And so, after two relatively expensive and ambitious productions with strong British connections, Hitch probably felt it was time to break free of this pattern. In addition, this project provided a good opportunity to demonstrate that he was capable of shooting a film in the studio quickly and cheaply.

Mr and Mrs Smith, like many of the screwball comedies of the late 1930s and early 1940s, could accurately be classified as a 'comedy of remarriage'. These movies typically revolved around a married couple who have become divorced, separated or 'unmarried' for some other reason, though they still love each other. Their crazy love-hate, off-on relationship constitutes the main subject of the film. The wife generally has a bland new boyfriend – Ralph Bellamy specialized in such parts – but he can never be regarded as serious competition for her sophisticated and charming husband, most often played by Cary Grant, as in *The Awful Truth* and *My Favourite Wife* and the closely related *His Girl Friday* and *The Philadelphia Story*. Grant was Hitchcock's first choice for the husband here too, though the role eventually went to Robert Montgomery. He probably better fits the script's 'all-American' premise that the couple were teenage sweethearts from a little town on the Idaho-Nevada border who now find that, due to a technicality, their marriage is not legally valid.

Montgomery and Lombard make an entertaining pair, acting out their own private war of the sexes, while the love-hate relationship between them escalates when she becomes involved with his business associate and partner, a dull Southern gentleman type played by Gene Raymond. There is never any doubt, however, that the couple will be back together again by the final fade out.

The film proved to be a suitable vehicle for Carole Lombard as the beautiful, but neurotic and insecure, wife whose behaviour, when she learns that they are not married, provides the main focus for the comedy. He, however, treats the situation as a bit of a joke, and is not in a hurry to get remarried. He unscrupulously employs every possible tactic to win her back – lying, cheating and playing ill – while she takes it very seriously indeed and appears to lose much of her former self-confidence and self-respect. The film also provided Lombard with ample opportunity to demonstrate her special gift for verbal, as well as physical, knockabout comedy. At one point, an elderly official from their town recalls her when she was young: 'She once chased a dog-catcher half a mile with a baseball bat.' To which Montgomery, her husband, replies, 'Maybe she hasn't changed all that much.'

For the second of his RKO movies, Hitchcock immediately followed *Mr and Mrs Smith* with another study of a youngish couple in *Suspicion*, adapted from the Frances Iles novel *Before the Fact*. This time he *did* get Cary Grant for the husband – the first of their four films together. Here Hitchcock returned to the psychological suspense story with a

One of the lighter moments early in *Suspicion* (1940) when Cary Grant arrives home with gifts for everyone claiming that he has just made a killing at the races. (Left to right): Joan Fontaine, Cary Grant, Nigel Bruce the family friend, and Heather Angel the maid. The stills photographer has captured here a hint of the young wife beginning to be troubled by the unpredictable behaviour of her new husband.

British setting reminiscent of *Rebecca*, and again Joan Fontaine was cast as the young wife. But on this film she and Hitch got on less well. She found him less supportive than on *Rebecca*, perhaps due in part to the fact that she was now a major star, and she wasn't happy with Cary either. In addition, various problems with the script meant that filming dragged on longer than it should have: over schedule and over budget, the picture ended up costing only slightly less than the far more expensive looking *Rebecca* and was a cause of considerable concern to the RKO executives. With Hitch serving virtually as his own producer, he was naturally regarded as the one most responsible. Once again, questions were raised regarding the slowness of his filming compared with that of the typical contract director. Yet all was forgiven once the picture was released. Though less impressive than *Rebecca*, *Suspicion* did turn out to be a big hit and provided a further boost to Hitch's reputation in Hollywood. It gained him yet another Oscar nomination for Best Picture, while Joan Fontaine was awarded the Oscar she should have won the previous year when she lost out to Ginger Rogers.

The film tells of the romance and subsequent marriage of a likeable, handsome playboy, played by Cary Grant, who is also an incorrigible liar and a bit of a villain, to a naïve young girl. She has vivid imagination and an unsophisticated view of the world, formed mainly through books. We are led to identify with her in her attraction to Grant in the opening reels and in much of the rest of the film. In fact, the picture starts off as light-hearted and entertaining in tone, a romantic comedy really, following on from *Mr and Mrs Smith*. The unpredictable off-again, on-again development of their relationship at first is followed by a whirlwind courtship, elopement and marriage, and it is only when they return from their honeymoon that she learns for the first time that he has no money of his own at all.

The picture is almost half over before the central theme, of 'suspicion', first begins to emerge. When her romantic notions start to turn a bit sour, it is not long before his endearingly spontaneous and irresponsible behaviour starts to look very different. (Cary Grant's performance strikes just the right note of superficial charm, but with hints of a darker, sinister side hidden not far beneath the surface.) She becomes increasingly suspicious of him even though most of her wild imaginings turn out to have little real foundation. However, it is not long before she has become so disturbed that she even suspects him of trying to kill her.

Hitchcock introduces an important new character fairly late in the film, a celebrated lady mystery writer (in the Agatha Christie mould) who lives nearby. With her forensic scientist brother present, the conversation over dinner becomes increasingly morbid as they animatedly discuss the best way to commit the perfect murder and whether there exists a poison that leaves no trace afterwards – further stimulating the heroine's darkest fears. (A neat expression here of Hitch's macabre sense of humour and a sequence that perfectly anticipates *Shadow of a Doubt* the following year.)

By this time, the whole tone of the film has changed quite considerably from the opening reels. Even the heroine's own house starts to look slightly sinister. One becomes more aware of the shadows on the walls and a lower-keyed lighting of scenes, leading up to the famous sequence when Grant brings her a bedtime glass of milk, which she fears may be poisoned. (This is shown in an effective high-angle view of the dim hallway and staircase at night: Grant approaches carrying the glass of milk. Hitchcock actually concealed a light bulb inside the glass to make it glow slightly, an effect that he was especially proud of.)

In his interview with Truffaut, Hitchcock apparently confused the ending found in the original novel with the one he had planned for his film and many critics have subsequently referred to *Suspicion* as an example of him being forced to compromise in Hollywood. In fact, according to Spoto, the original ending, in which the husband actually poisons his wife, was regarded as a serious problem in adapting the book at RKO. But Hitch, early on, had agreed to change this, 'making the husband's deeds the fictions in the mind of a neurotically suspicious woman'. Thus, the ending, as filmed, works well and certainly fits in better with the main theme than if the husband really was a murderer. In the film's new final sequence she thinks he is trying to push her out of their speeding car when, in fact, he's trying to save her, having noticed that the door is not properly shut – yet one more example of her irrational fears. In this portrait of a mismatched couple, it is clear that their many misunderstandings are almost as much her fault as his – his secrecy and irresponsibility matched by her vivid imaginings. When the couple return to the house at the end after a reconciliation has taken place, it is difficult to be optimistic about their future together.

After directing two films that were totally removed from the current world situation, Hitch was once again ready to return to a topical thriller format, as he had previously done with *Foreign Correspondent* a year and a half earlier. The US had still not entered the war, and the outlook for Britain was extremely bleak. At least through a strongly anti-Nazi picture, he could make his own modest contribution to the war effort. He himself suggested the original story idea for the film, to be called *Saboteur*, and it was first developed as a possible third project for RKO, adapting the pattern of the chase thriller that he had used so effectively in such British films as *The 39 Steps* and *Young and Innocent*. But Hitchcock ended up at Universal instead.

His deal at Universal provides yet another example of the kind of changes that were taking place in Hollywood around this time and the role played by Hitchcock himself. Whereas Universal had previously produced all its own pictures, the studio was now making a special effort to improve their quality, negotiating its first deals with leading independent producers in 1941. For example, Walter Wanger was hired by Universal at about the same time that Selznick had signed the contract to loan them Hitchcock.

By mid-1941, Hitchcock had achieved a leading status in Hollywood – in spite of the fact that his name was still most closely associated with the suspense or thriller genre – and Universal could regard its contract with him as a real coup. He himself appears to have been less bothered by the move from RKO to the rather less classy Universal studio, than by his failure to get the cast he wanted for his first film there. (He was forced to settle for Universal star Robert Cummings, and Priscilla Lane, who had just been released by Warner Bros.) In fact, this was the only period in his entire Hollywood career that he would work for one of the smaller and less prestigious companies. (By the time he returned to Universal in the early 1960s, the company had become one of the leading studios.)

Saboteur starts off dramatically as a young aircraft worker (Robert Cummings) witnesses an act of sabotage and a spectacular fire at the factory where he works in southern California. Though he has a good idea who the culprits are, he himself has been framed by them and just manages to escape. We naturally identify with him in his subsequent efforts to clear himself and catch the real saboteurs, a task that takes him on a cross-country journey by way of Boulder Dam to New York City. Along the way he encounters a random cross-section of Americans, including an elderly blind man, a sympathetic truck driver, and a group of circus performers on a train. Some are helpful and others are not. He crashes a charity ball held by New York socialites and develops an up and down relationship with an attractive girl whom he keeps meeting and losing. Her uncle is the leader of the gang of fifth columnists, which makes it difficult for him to convince her of his own innocence.

Although frustrated in his choice of stars, the episodic structure of the film at least allowed Hitchcock to make use of a generous selection of Hollywood bit players – but here given an appropriately Hitchcockian twist. For the hero never knows whom he can trust. (A nice elderly gentleman first seen playing with his granddaughter turns out to be the chief villain, and at one point a little old lady housekeeper takes him, and us, by surprise when she suddenly produces a small gun from her purse.)

Best remembered of all are the set-piece sequences near the end. When Fry, the leading saboteur, escapes into the Radio City Music Hall, his silhouette is dwarfed by the giant movie screen. The dramatic chase and real gunshots are matched by the dialogue, action and gunfire in the movie being projected to an audience who remain unaware of anything unusual going on. The final confrontation takes place at the top of the Statue of Liberty where the hero finally catches up with Fry. In a hair-raising sequence Fry dangles as the hero attempts to pull him to safety, clutching at the arm of his jacket. He watches helplessly as it slowly comes away at the seams, and Fry falls to his death.

The completed picture was less than Hitchcock at his best. Aside from the weaknesses of the stars, Lane in particular, the plot was a bit too loosely structured, and Hitchcock himself later admitted that he had not been entirely satisfied with the screenplay before he was forced to begin filming. In addition, there are a few patriotic speeches inserted at various points, which fulfilled the film's propoganda role, but look a bit embarrassing in retrospect.

Yet it was entertaining and proved popular with audiences at the time, probably benefiting from the fact that it was one of the first anti-Nazi pictures to be released after the US entered the war. (Much of the film had actually been shot *before* Pearl Harbor, during the late autumn and winter of 1941.)

Following the success of *Saboteur*, Hitchcock was immediately given the opportunity to make a second picture at Universal. After three years (and five features) in Hollywood, the time was right for him to try something a bit less conventional. He had discovered an especially interesting and original idea for his next picture that did not require any elaborate sets or special effects or big stars. (It had been suggested to him by Gordon McDonell, the husband of one of Selznick's story editors.)

It obviously did not matter to him that he was at one of the smaller of the Hollywood majors, working with budgets of under $1 million, for the new project would be entirely under his own control – as long as he stayed within the agreed budget. Note, too, that whereas at RKO he had chosen to film two of the studio's own properties, at Universal he was able to develop a pair of original film ideas of his own. At only $800,000, his new picture, originally called, 'Uncle Charlie', but later retitled *Shadow of a Doubt*, was planned as the lowest costing of all his American films. An intimate, small-scale subject and relatively modest by Hollywood standards, this would be his first opportunity to make a truly American picture exactly as he envisaged it, with his leading male star playing a psychotic murderer.

He was determined to bring to the screen his own personal view of small town America – rather different from that version found in countless other Hollywood movies of the period. As he noted at the time, 'I am extremely anxious to avoid the conventional small town American scene. By conventional I mean the stock figures that have been seen in so many films of this type. I would like them to be very modern . . .' He even managed to find exactly the small town he was looking for in Northern California 50 miles north of San Francisco and planned to shoot all the exteriors on location rather than on the studio back lot (where it would have been easier for the studio bosses to keep a closer eye on him).

A strong advocate of location filming whenever possible, this was the
first time in the US that he scouted locations with his writer before they
began work on the screenplay – a procedure that he would follow in
many of his later American films in the 1950s. Hitch recalled, '. . . the
writer, Thornton Wilder, and I went and stayed in the town, [Santa
Rosa, California] lived in it, got to know the people . . . and came back
and wrote the script based on the people and nature and character of the
town itself.'

Effectively functioning as his own producer, Hitchcock was able to
assemble an outstanding cast and crew and established a congenial
environment for filming on location in the summer of 1942 (another
notable first for him). According to the film's star, Teresa Wright, the

Hitchcock is seen here with his wife, Alma Reville, his life-long companion
and collaborator who worked on many of his films, often as a scriptwriter or
uncredited script consultant. They first met at the very beginning of his
movie career, in 1921, when she was already an experienced continuity girl
and editor. They were married in 1926, and she continued to contribute to
virtually all of his pictures throughout his long career.

production got off to an excellent start. 'During the shooting he made us feel very relaxed . . . We felt we could trust him, and he gave us guidance and a sense of freedom . . . We were the first film company to work in Santa Rosa, and everyone there got involved in one way or another. Everyone was wonderful to us, even when our nighttime shooting interrupted their quiet routine.' These remarks were echoed by her co-star, Joseph Cotten, who insisted that 'no director was ever easier to work with'.

The crew was headed by cameraman Joseph Valentine and art director Robert Boyle, both of whom had been with Hitch on *Saboteur* the previous year. Boyle was just beginning a long and distinguished career as a production designer and found working with Hitch 'extremely rewarding and instructive . . . I find Hitch a catalyst to my own creative functioning,' he wrote many years later. 'He is one of the few who really knows the materials of his craft and their effect.' (They would renew their association in the late 1950s and early 1960s when Boyle served as art director on three of Hitchcock's later features beginning with *North by Northwest*.)

In fact, the town itself plays an important role in *Shadow of a Doubt*. Eager to avoid the kind of cliché that suggests that nasty things are only apt to happen on dark and deserted streets at night, Hitchcock's wicked sense of humour pushed him in the opposite direction. He was fond of demonstrating, in many of his films, that nastiness and evil could be found within normal, everyday settings. Thus, in *Shadow of a Doubt* he exploits the contrast between the darker side of the story, represented by the mysterious Uncle Charlie, played by Joseph Cotten, and the relatively innocent and uneventful day-to-day life in a small, close-knit American community, which he brilliantly captures on the screen. (Thornton Wilder proved to be an inspired choice as scriptwriter, hired by Hitchcock following his play and 1940 film version of *Our Town*.)

In the film's prologue, Hitchcock makes use of some audacious cross-cutting to establish an almost telepathic link between young Charlie, played by Teresa Wright, at her home in California, and the uncle she idolizes, on the run from the police, far across the continent, on the East Coast. The story proper only begins when he arrives to visit the family. (Her mother is his older sister.) Young Charlie's natural curiosity leads to suspicion and then confirmation of her favourite uncle's unsavoury past. There is an echo of the central relationship in *Suspicion* here, except that, in this case, he really *is* a murderer and does try to murder her, and make it look like an 'accident'. She, however, finds it impossible to tell the other members of the family, up to the very end when she accidentally causes his death and he is, ironically, given a hero's funeral.

Here Hitchcock was especially well served by his large cast, from the two stars to the many excellent character actors and bit players, some recruited from the residents of the real town. Joseph Cotten's performance cleverly suggests the psychotic tension hidden beneath the charming and sophisticated exterior. 'He said I should dress as if I were a rich man going to a resort for a vacation.' His character emerged as the first in a long line of memorable Hitchcock villains to be found in many of the best of his American films. Similarly, Teresa Wright was excellent as the sensitive and vulnerable young heroine. Here Hitchcock put her wholesome, 'girl-next-door' image to good use, and she responded, conveying a very real sense of her character's maturing during the course of the film. Young Charlie proves to be a resourceful and intelligent young lady, and Hitchcock also managed to get the balance just right between her and Cotten at the core of the picture.

Joseph Cotten (right) plays the sympathetic uncle in *Shadow of a Doubt* (1943) while Teresa Wright (centre) finds it hard to tell her mother (Patricia Collinge) of her suspicion that he is really a serial murderer on the run from the police, and that her own life may be in danger. This picture marked Hitchcock's first notable attempt to capture the feel of American small-town life on the screen.

He was equally successful in filling in the other characters, too, deftly sketching in the various members of the slightly eccentric Newton family – the extremely studious qualities, a bit unexpected, in the tiny, youngest girl; her younger brother, equally obsessed with mathematics; and the black humour of the two harmless old men who never tire of arguing over how to commit the perfect murder. They, like the fussy, doting mother, are blissfully unaware of the drama being acted out between the two Charlies, which makes the plight of the young heroine that much more unbearable.

In addition to including many nicely observed visual details of small town life, the use of sound in the picture is quite exceptional. Here Hitchcock experimented with different ways of capturing the feel of this diverse little household, where everyone talks and no one listens. The microphone is used to pick up fragments of dialogue as the characters move from room to room, with bits of overlapping or 'throwaway' lines, as Hitchcock allows them to interrupt each other or to speak at the same time while ensuring that essential bits come through clearly.

Filmed in the summer and autumn of 1942, *Shadow of a Doubt* qualifies as one of the earliest entries in the cycle of forties *film noir*. At the same time it also stands out as one of Hitchcock's most personal and memorable pictures, and one of his own personal favourites. He had achieved a special kind of resonance here in exploring the dark, sinister and morally ambiguous *noir* themes within an innocent small town setting, rather than the more usual big city milieu. As Donald Spoto has noted, 'it is a profoundly disturbing tale . . . It is a *film noir* that marked a major shift in the director's tone', and from this point on 'there is a moral cynicism about the human condition that pervades all his best work.'

Suddenly Hitchcock found that he was in good company and that many other leading Hollywood directors had been attracted to the thriller genre around this same time. Reflecting the increasingly pessimistic, cynical mood of the war years and the immediate postwar period, and a general disillusionment with traditional American attitudes and values, many of the directors, and especially those from the new generation of American and/or European emigrés, found that they could achieve a more personal style of filming and even deal with a range of contemporary social themes, within the psychological thriller or suspense format. There was, in fact, a major upgrading of the entire crime movie genre as it was reclaimed from the cheap 'B' movies and studio programmers of 1930s Hollywood. The scripts were better, often adapted from leading writers such as Hammett, Chandler or James M. Cain, and the films drew on the expertise of top cameramen, art directors, sound recordists and other technicians as an important part of the last great era of black-and-white filming. No longer constricted within the typical B-movie running time of 75 minutes or less, they could give considered attention to subtleties of characterization and relationships, create a mood on the screen and capture the feel of a setting or milieu, aided by the trend towards more filming on location.

In his cultural history of American movies, *Movie-Made America*, Robert Sklar drew attention to Hitchcock's special contribution: '*Film noir* seems to have been especially nurtured by the macabre imagination of the British director Alfred Hitchcock . . . The Hitchcock thriller, in its fascination with guilt and its ambiguous play with identities, served as a prototype for *film noir* in such movies as *Suspicion* : . . [and] *Shadow of a Doubt* [which] was one of the transcendent works of the genre . . .' Other leading new directors who made a major contribution to *film noir* during the early 1940s included Orson Welles (with *Citizen Kane* (1941) as an obvious precurser; he also produced *Journey into Fear* in 1942); John Huston (*The Maltese Facon*, 1941); Billy Wilder (*Double Indemnity*, 1943) and Robert Siodmak (*Phantom Lady*, 1943). Edward Dmytryk (*Farewell my Lovely/Murder my Sweet*, 1944) and Otto Preminger (*Laura*, 1944). But Hitchcock alone was most closely identified with this type of film and thus benefited most from the changing attitudes to the genre. He would continue to play a major role in the *noir* cycle during the following years, directing some of his most memorable films, including *Notorious* (1946), on which he was officially credited as producer and director for the first time, and *Strangers on a Train* (1951). From now on he would be working with top Hollywood stars, such as Ingrid Bergman, Cary Grant, Gregory Peck and James Stewart. In addition, he would feature prominently on the list of top hits in 1946 when the cycle was at its box office peak. (Both *Spellbound* and *Notorious* were in the top ten with rentals of over $4.5 million each; *The Postman Always Rings Twice* and *Gilda* also made the top twenty and the dozen or so *noir* hits in the top sixty, with rentals over $2.25 million, included *The Big Sleep* and *The Blue Dahlia* from Raymond Chandler, *The Killers*, from Hemingway, directed by Siodmak, and the biggest ever hits from Fritz Lang (*Scarlet Street* and *Cloak and Dagger*) and Orson Welles (*The Stranger*).

4

1943-47:
War Films and Selznick Again

From *Lifeboat* to *The Paradine Case*

By early 1943, after slightly less than four active years in Hollywood, Hitchcock had completed six features. He had experienced a remarkable degree of success during these years, not least at the box office where five of his six features had been profitable, especially *Rebecca* and *Suspicion*. (With profits of almost half a million dollars, *Suspicion* was RKO's biggest hit of 1941.) *Foreign Correspondent*, the most expensive, was the only one to record a small loss.

Under contract to Selznick, who had given up producing pictures for a few years, but continued to pay him his regular salary, Hitchcock's standing in Hollywood was clearly reflected in the kind of fees that Selznick was able to get by loaning out his services to other studios. In 1939, his initial weekly salary of $2,500 had appeared generous, and the best offer he had received from Hollywood. But by 1940–1, Selznick was already loaning him to Wanger and then to RKO for twice that amount (and pocketing the difference himself). The going rate for Hitchcock's services soon escalated to $9,000 per week at Universal and then at 20th Century-Fox, while Hitchcock's own salary only rose to $3,000. (The Fox deal, however, was the last time that Hitch was loaned out in this way.)

Although he was understandably unhappy over the fact that he received only a small share of the large fees that the studios were paying Selznick, at least Hitchcock could console himself with the fact that he was able to function with a large degree of creative freedom, and he was still one of the more highly paid of Hollywood directors. (His earnings rose from $137,000 in 1939 to $157,000 in 1940 and $176,000 in 1941–2 including bonuses.) Also, by making films at a number of different studios under different working conditions he had been able to familiarize himself very quickly with the Hollywood system. In addition, he often received a salary bonus from Selznick or the studio when a film was successful. (He got $15,000 from Universal for *Saboteur*, for example.) But there was no bonus for *Lifeboat*, his only picture for Fox, which also turned out to be his most expensive and troubled production of the early 1940s. (He was originally meant to complete two films in the time taken by this one.)

As with *Shadow of a Doubt*, Hitchcock had the idea of collaborating with a leading American writer, John Steinbeck, on an original film subject. But in marked contrast to *Shadow of a Doubt*, and in keeping with his own preference for never repeating himself, *Lifeboat* was conceived as a totally studio-bound production. Returning to the wartime theme, he was attracted to the challenge of shooting the entire film in and around a single lifeboat floating at sea, showing the experiences of a group of survivors from a torpedoed ship in the Atlantic. Hitchcock himself has referred to the film as a 'microcosm of the war', and his comments suggest that this is the one picture that was conceived and developed primarily to dramatize a particular propaganda theme: 'We wanted to show that at that moment there were two world forces confronting each other, the democracies and the Nazis, and while the democracies were completely disorganized, all of the Germans were clearly headed in the same direction. So here was a statement telling the democracies to put their differences aside temporarily and to gather their forces to concentrate on the common enemy . . .'

Bearing this in mind, one can readily accept the picture as a superbly crafted piece of propaganda, which unfortunately does not stand up so well as a film, being more 'literary' than cinematic in format, with a rather too obviously calculated cross-section of characters. They tend to appear as the representatives of a particular viewpoint – one left-wing crew member, one sympathetic black, a sophisticated lady journalist, a rich businessman, a young army nurse, one German survivor of the Nazi U-boat, etc., among the group of nine – rather than as individuals. In addition, there were obvious weaknesses in the script and dialogue. But at least Hitchcock got along well with his leading actress, stage star Tallulah Bankhead, who played the journalist and gave perhaps the best if characteristically over-the-top, performance (for which she won the New York Film Critics award) of her brief and intermittent movie career.

Lifeboat caused some controversy at the time it was released, since the Nazi came across as the most resourceful of the group. This was not at all surprising, as he was an experienced seaman. But Hitchcock was making the point here that the Allies should not underestimate their enemy. In any case, the film ended up as Hitchcock's most expensive of the early 1940s, took in less at the box office and thus was his first real

John Hodiak (out of shot) objects to the fact that their German prisoner (Walter Slezak) appears to have taken command of the boat, provoking a quick reaction from the other survivors in this scene from *Lifeboat* (1944). (Left to right): Hume Cronyn and Mary Anderson below, Slezak at the oars, Henry Hull, Canada Lee and the injured William Bendix (back to camera). They fail to realize that Hodiak's suspicions are correct and that they are heading toward a German supply ship rather than Bermuda, and safety.

American flop. He had spent almost exactly a year on the film, which he was meant to complete in half that time. (It undoubtedly would have done better if completed and released earlier in the war, in 1943 rather than 1944 when the tide of war was already swinging strongly in the Allies' favour; and by this time, movie audiences had also been subjected to rather too many war pictures.)

Lifeboat's serious theme, however, appealed to the members of the Academy and Hitchcock received his second Oscar nomination for directing, while Steinbeck's original story and Glen MacWilliams' cinematography were also recognized. This was in marked contrast to the relative neglect of *Shadow of a Doubt* the previous year, which had received a single nomination only, for the original story.

This was perhaps an appropriate time for Hitchcock to take a short break from Hollywood. At the very end of 1943, he was invited to London by Sidney Bernstein to make a further contribution to the war effort by directing two propaganda shorts for the British Ministry of Information (MOI). Filmed in French at the Welwyn Studios early in 1944, both featured a group of French refugee actors known as the Molière Players. *Aventure Malagache* depicted the activities of the French resistance on the island of Madagascar, while *Bon Voyage* was a spy thriller about an escaped British POW (a Scots sergeant) whose fellow escaper is revealed as a Gestapo agent and is killed. (Hitchcock would return to London early in the summer of 1945, again at Sidney Bernstein's request, to work on a feature length, Anglo-American co-production on the Nazi concentration camps; it was virtually completed before the project was abandoned in the autumn of 1945.)

At the same time that Hitchcock was involved with *Lifeboat*, in 1943, David Selznick had finally made his long overdue return to active film-making. Just over three years had elapsed from the completion of post-production work on *Rebecca* (in February 1940) to the spring of 1943 when he had begun writing the script adaptation for *Since You Went Away*, his 'comeback' movie for 1944. Around the same time he had become interested in psychoanalysis, having been in analysis briefly himself, and had discussed with Hitch the idea of doing a film to take advantage of the current widespread interest in this subject. With this in mind, Hitchcock himself had bought the rights to a novel, *The House of Dr Edwardes* by Francis Beeding, while he was in England early in 1943, and began work on an initial treatment with writer Angus Mac-Phail, who had scripted his two documentary shorts.

Back in the US, Hitch collaborated closely with leading scriptwriter Ben Hecht, who had been in analysis too, and it soon became clear that Selznick was planning to produce the picture himself, casting the lead roles from his own list of contract stars. Most important of all, this would be Hitch's first opportunity to direct Selznick's fastest rising female star, Ingrid Bergman. Both Hitchcock and Bergman had arrived in the US at the same time, in the spring of 1939, brought to Hollywood by Selznick, but not long after this Selznick had stopped producing and loaned them out instead. Cast in some less than memorable films initially, Bergman's success during 1942–4 had been quite remarkable. The Oscar-winning *Casablanca* was followed by *For Whom the Bell Tolls*; she was Oscar nominated for her performance, and she won the following year with *Gaslight*. She and Hitchcock would make three films together during 1944–8 when she was at her peak in popularity – rated the leading female (dramatic) star at the box office.

The first of their three films, *Spellbound*, looks very much like a Bergman star vehicle. She is rarely off the screen, and is the only woman with more than a tiny role. (Rhonda Fleming makes a brief appearance as a provocative young lady patient.) In fact, the extended cast list includes only four women out of twenty-eight listed roles. At the mental hospital where the film opens, Bergman is the attractive young psychiatrist among a virtually all-male staff, and through the course of the film, with one notable exception, there is a succession of middle-aged or elderly men, including almost all of the bit players, sheriff, detectives, a hotel house detective and even a middle-aged drunk (Wallace Ford) who tries to pick her up in a hotel lobby, where Hitchcock makes his familiar cameo appearance. The film is almost stolen by the elderly psychiatrist played by Michael Chekhov.

With this in mind, it is surprising to learn that Joseph Cotten was the first actor considered for the leading male role by Selznick and Hitchcock. This casting would have created a very different balance at the centre of the film from the one that eventually emerged. Rather than a relatively sophisticated and experienced older man – Cotten was ten years older than Bergman – Gregory Peck, who was eventually cast in the role, comes across as young and vulnerable. (He was exactly a year younger than she and relatively new to films, this being his third feature.) His character is seriously disturbed in a manner very different from Uncle Charlie of *Shadow of a Doubt*. Suffering from amnesia and a serious guilt complex and thinking he may himself be a murderer, he becomes extremely dependent on Bergman during the course of the film. In an unusually strong female role for a Hitchcock movie, she is characterized throughout by her intelligence, energy and strength, and she alone uncovers and confronts the real murderer at the end of the film. The youthful and handsome Peck clearly stands out from the rest of the cast. It is not surprising that Bergman falls in love with him, and it is difficult to imagine how the relationship would have developed with Cotten instead.

The idea of Hitchcock making a film about psychoanalysis at this point in his career sounds intriguing. However, the picture took shape as a relatively conventional and 'novelettish', if well made, Hollywood love story, recalling *Rebecca* more strongly than any of the other Hitchcock films in between. In short, another Selznick picture. This sense of disappointment is obviously shared by François Truffaut: '. . . one expects a Hitchcock film on psychoanalysis to be wildly imaginative – way out! Instead, this turns out to be one of your most sensible pictures . . . rather weak on fantasy.' This is especially surprising in that, whereas, on *Rebecca*, Hitch and his writers were forced to remain faithful to the original novel, there were no such pressures from Selznick on *Spellbound*, which was virtually a film original, with very little retained from the book. In fact, Hitch and Hecht were allowed to develop the script without any interference from Selznick who was preoccupied with post-production problems, release details and publicity for *Since You Went Away*, his long-awaited comeback film, which had gone far over schedule and over budget.

In addition, Hitchcock was in a much stronger position now than on *Rebecca*, more confident about his status in Hollywood than when he had first arrived five years earlier, whereas Selznick was less secure in his role as producer and had lost many of the key personnel at his studio during the years of inactivity (and his marriage of fourteen years was in trouble, too). This was most clearly reflected in Hitchcock's refusal to let Selznick interfere in any way with the filming. Selznick later referred to the fact that he was hardly ever on the set as an example of his 'great respect for Hitchcock', but this is contradicted by Ingrid Bergman. She recalled that Hitchcock simply stopped the cameras whenever Selznick appeared.

Apparently, Hitchcock's most imaginative ideas concerned the dream sequences, and it was his idea to hire Salvador Dali to design them. As originally filmed by him, the dreams were quite remarkable, according to Ingrid Bergman, '. . . a wonderful, twenty-minute sequence that belongs in a museum. The idea for a major part of it was that I would become, in Gregory Peck's mind, a statue . . . I was dressed in a draped, Grecian gown, with a crown on my head and an arrow through my neck . . .' It is difficult to see how such a long sequence would have fitted into the film. It was, in fact, considerably shortened and re-edited into four separate sections as part of Selznick's post-production contribution.

In his interview with Hitchcock, Truffaut draws attention to one of the few other imaginative touches specially injected into the film – the corridor shot, with doors opening into the distance as the couple kiss for the first time. (Here, and elewhere in the film, one can detect a slightly tongue-in-cheek attitude on Hitchcock's part.) Truffaut also liked the first meeting between the couple, 'that was so clearly love at first sight'. 'Unfortunately, the violins begin to play just then,' Hitchcock reminds him. 'That was terrible.'

The over use of background music was one of Selznick's contributions to the final film. A romantic love theme is contrasted with the music, including the high-pitched, eerie sound of the theremin, used by composer Miklos Rozsa to announce that Peck is about to experience another one of his severe mental blocks. The scoring of the picture, as well as the final edit, was supervised by Selznick, as he had done on *Rebecca* and his other features. Known for his meticulous attention to detail and for his ability to recognize and remedy any weaknesses during the post-production phase of filming, Selznick would even have his director and cast reshoot sequences if he felt it would improve the film, in spite of the added expense. *Spellbound*, in fact, represented an extremely rare example of a Selznick picture on which he had had virtually no involvement during the filming; so, in spite of the shooting having gone extremely smoothly, completed well within schedule, it was inevitable that Selznick would find plenty to do. There was some additional filming, including a new, improved ending with a giant prop gun, and various other retakes, as well as the usual attention to scoring and some re-editing, based in part on the reactions of preview audiences.

This dragged on through most of 1945. Once the picture was completed to Selznick's satisfaction, there was the dilemma of making sure that it was released at just the right time. He finally organized a lavish

Ingrid Bergman was Hitchcock's favourite star of the 1940s. In *Spellbound* (1945), the first of their three films together, she played a psychiatrist who becomes romantically involved with a disturbed young man (and murder suspect) played by Gregory Peck. A tremendous hit for producer David O. Selznick, the picture brought together Selznick's three leading contract personnel of the decade – Bergman, Peck and director Hitchcock.

premiere on Hallowe'en night, one year after Hitchcock had completed principal photography. The film now had to compete with two other Bergman films released at the same time – *The Bells of St Mary's* (from RKO) and *Saratoga Trunk* (filmed at Warner Bros two years earlier). However, she had won the Oscar earlier in the year, as the adverts for *Spellbound* would make clear, and such was her appeal that all three were big hits. *The Bells of St Mary's*, co-starring Bing Crosby, was not only the top film of the year, but the most profitable ever produced by RKO; similarly, with its relatively modest cost of $1.7 million and profits of $2 million, *Spellbound* proved to be Selznick's most profitable black-and-white picture (topped only by *Gone with the Wind* and *Duel in the Sun*) and UA's most successful of the 1940s. In addition, *Spellbound* turned out to be the last Selznick production to be nominated for the Best Picture Oscar, while Hitchcock gained his third directing nomination. Other nominations were for George Barnes' cinematography (he had previously won for *Rebecca*), Michael Chekhov for best supporting actor, and special effects. Rozsa emerged as the only winner, for his score. Bergman and Peck were both nominated for their performances in their previously completed films, *The Bells of St Mary's* and *The Keys of the Kingdom*, respectively.

Whereas five years earlier the opening titles had read, 'The Selznick studio presents its production of Daphne du Maurier's *Rebecca*', now Hitchcock was credited 'above the title' for the first time: 'David O. Selznick (in small letters) presents Ingrid Bergman and Gregory Peck in Alfred Hitchcock's *Spellbound*'. But this did not change Hitchcock's slightly dismissive view of the film, best summed up in his comment to Truffaut: 'Well, it's just another manhunt story wrapped up in pseudo-psychoanalysis.'

Of course, there is no way that Hitchcock could have anticipated the tremendous success of *Spellbound*, yet he had been aware at the time that there had been an unusually long gap between his films, and the disappointment of *Lifeboat* meant that he could really use a hit. His work on *Rebecca* was made more tolerable by the knowledge that he would have much more freedom on his next film, *Foreign Correspondent*. Similarly, the success of *Saboteur* had given him the opportunity to make *Shadow of a Doubt* at the same studio. Now returning to direct his first film for Selznick in five years, he had recognized the need to make *Spellbound* a successful *Selznick* picture in order to be able to go on and do the film he really wanted to do.

In fact, Hitchcock and Hecht had first become interested in the idea that would develop into their next film together, *Notorious*, while they were still working on *Spellbound*. Hitchcock hoped to be able to make another picture with Bergman, at this time planning to cast her in the role of a 'loose woman', mixing a romantic story with an espionage or confidence trick theme.

Selznick, too, was involved in this new project from the very beginning and appeared likely to produce it. Again, as with *Spellbound*, he made various suggestions, but generally left Hitchcock and Hecht to write the script. Thus, they began work on it soon after Hitchcock had completed principal photography on *Spellbound* and long before that film was released. By late spring, Selznick had already begun casting. The idea of teaming Bergman with Cary Grant for the first time required some additional re-working of the script to expand his role. As it developed, the story would revolve around a woman forced to go to bed with a second man and then to marry him as part of her professional duties. Once it was agreed that the film would benefit from a strong performance in this part, Claude Rains was chosen to complete the film's line-up of stars.

At the same time that this new project was taking shape, Selznick was becoming increasingly involved with his current production in the summer of 1945, *Duel in the Sun*, an epic, Technicolor Western starring Jennifer Jones. Faced with various problems, rapidly escalating costs and the need to inject additional funds, he finally decided to sell the entire *Notorious* package, including Hitchcock, script and stars, if he could get a good price. He negotiated first with producer Hal Wallis, but then turned to RKO where he finalised a deal in July. He would receive $800,000 immediately and a 50 per cent share in any profits.

The departure of Selznick meant that Hitchcock would be allowed to produce and direct – the first American film on which he would be officially credited as producer. He would be able to control every aspect of the picture from the scripting stage through to filming and post-production. Thus, it is not surprising (and is quite revealing) to see how differently *Notorious* would turn out, in spite of the fact that it had also originated from the same team of Selznick, Hitchcock, Hecht and Bergman. And it was also conceived by Hitchcock as being quite different from his own, previously most original contribution to forties *film noir*, *Shadow of a Doubt*. Whereas in that film he had attempted to capture the interaction of a family within a small town setting by filming on location, *Notorious* was devised by Hitchcock as a studio-based star vehicle of a very special kind. With three leading stars and above the line costs already approaching the $1 million mark before the film even went into production, there was a danger that his first feature as producer would be a money-loser – recalling his experience on *Foreign Correspondent* – if costs were not kept under control. But whereas that film had required many elaborate sets and special effects, depending on the specialized skills of designers and technicians, in *Notorious* he aimed for a simplicity and economy of style that could be achieved with a regular team of RKO studio personnel, with no need for any special outside assistance. The only person specially brought in was Paramount's top costume designer, Edith Head, who supplied the many stylish gowns required for Miss Bergman. Thus, below-the-line production costs would end up being very similar to those on *Spellbound* – (see table at the end of this chapter).

Hitchcock has often referred to the tremendous amount of time and effort that he devotes to the pre-planning and visualizing of his pictures prior to shooting – in some respects it is the most creative part of the film-making process for him. 'I plan out a script very carefully,' he wrote in 1938, 'hoping to follow it exactly all the way through when the shooting starts. This working on the script is the real making of the film, for me. When I've done it, the film is finished already in my mind.'

Notorious provided him with an ideal opportunity to develop this method in a very special way. Here he would attempt to achieve a particularly intense and intimate style by emphasizing close-ups and medium close-up shots in filming his stars, concentrating especially on the romance between Ingrid Bergman and Cary Grant. In the interior sequences, such as in the celebrated unbroken three-minute long embrace and kiss, all filmed in one take, and in shooting the exteriors as well – speeding along the highway alone at night or meeting at an outdoor café, at a racetrack or on a park bench – the backgrounds or settings are ignored as Hitchcock's interest centres on the interaction between Bergman and Grant to the exclusion of all else. Even the technique of back projection, generally used to reduce the costs of outdoor filming, serves a stylistic function here, bringing the characters closer to us and helping to preserve the intimacy of their relationship. The outside world is never allowed to intrude. They are always in sharp focus, and it does not matter that the world around them appears a bit fuzzy.

Hitchcock's special care with the look of the film however, did not mean neglecting the actors. On the contrary, all three leads are quite excellent. He managed to draw an intensely felt yet sensual performance from Bergman in particular, with a few obvious echoes of her previous roles: the 'loose girl' of *Dr Jekyll and Mr Hyde*; vulnerable and terrorized as in *Gaslight*; the intense, romantic involvement of *For Whom the Bell Tolls*; the romance and anti-Nazi intrigues of *Casablanca*. As one writer noted, she is in a semi-delirious state throughout much of the film, either sexually infatuated, half drunk, half poisoned or hung over

from the night before. Again, as in *Spellbound*, she is the lone young woman in a cast dominated by middle-aged or elderly men.

Cary Grant is perfectly cast as the cynical, but romantically inclined, intelligence agent. He recruits Bergman, the playgirl daughter of a convicted Nazi spy, to help infiltrate a group of Nazi conspirators who have relocated in South America after the war. When he becomes emotionally and sexually involved with her, he is unsure of himself and unwilling to trust his feelings for her. Her rapid success with Alex, the leader of the Nazis, played by Claude Rains, makes him a bit suspicious and cynical, in view of her past, while she feels extremely insecure and vulnerable and unsure what to do, especially once Rains has asked her to marry him. She wants Grant to tell her not to go through with it, but he, in turn, wants her to make up her own mind. Although he loves her, he is not eager to say so. Not only is it difficult for him to put his feelings into words, but also his professional role is mixed up in their relationship, and cancelling their undercover operation might involve some awkward explanations to his own superiors.

Faced with Grant's seemingly insensitive attitude, she no longer cares what happens to herself and agrees to proceed with the plans and marriage to Rains. Rains comes across as an appealing figure and one of the most fascinating, and fully characterized, of Hitchcock's villains. He portrays a rich and powerful businessman, attracted to Bergman and appearing genuinely in love and eager to marry her, in spite of the objections of his domineering, elderly mother. We can't help but feel a bit of sympathy for him at the end of the film, faced with almost certain death at the hands of his associates once it has become apparent that he has unwittingly married an American agent. The fourth remarkable performance comes from the veteran actress Leopoldine Konstantin, as Alex's formidable mother – jealous and suspicious at first regarding his plans to marry, then calculating and ruthless in planning and carrying out their revenge – death by slow poisoning.

Hitchcock fondly recalled this prolonged embrace and kiss between the two stars in *Notorious* (1946) as 'one of my most famous scenes'. This atmospheric photo also anticipates the intimate moment toward the end of the film when Cary Grant arrives in Ingrid Bergman's bedroom and his kiss helps her to summon up the strength to escape from the couple who are trying to poison her. (The picture proved to be Hitch's most memorable and successful 1940s production; the first time in Hollywood that he was officially credited as director *and* producer).

Throughout the first half of the film Hitchcock avoids the typically low-keyed photography and other stylized effects most often associated with forties *film noir*. Cameraman Ted Tetzlaff was best known for his work on musicals and comedies. (He would only briefly become identified with *noir* subjects as an RKO director in the late 1940s.) Thus, most of the film has the slightly glossy appearance of a major studio production of the period, mainly taking place among the smart set in sunny Rio. The few location and establishing shots were obviously filmed by a second unit. Hitchcock and his stars never left Hollywood.

As planned and filmed by him, the picture makes use of a relatively small number of settings. Most important of all is the wealthy Alex's well-lit and spacious mansion, which only begins to take on a slightly sinister tone late in the film, as had happened with the heroine's home in *Suspicion*. Both pictures were, in fact, designed by the same RKO team headed by art director Carroll Clark and set designer Darrell Silvera. First seen by us when Rains invites Bergman to dinner, we gain a special familiarity with the house as the plot thickens.

The entire ground floor is the setting for a lavish party, which opens with one of Hitchcock's most ingenious shots. Beginning with a long view of the main hallway from above, the camera descends, then moves in to a tight close-up of Bergman's hand clutching the key to the wine cellar. The tension mounts during the evening as she and Grant try to pick the right moment to slip away unnoticed to investigate the cellar below. When a wine bottle accidentally breaks, they discover that it is full of some kind of black metal powder. It is uranium oxide. Grant is able to take a sample with him, but they have no time to conceal the evidence, and Rains becomes suspicious when he sees them together.

Taking place midway through the film, the party marks a turning point in the plot and stylistically, too, the film takes on a more 'noirish' feel. When the worried Rains wakes up his mother to seek her advice, Hitchcock cuts to a low angle shot of the two of them in the dimly-lit bedroom. The camera is angled in such a way as to make it clear that she is now in the dominant position, while Rains looks very small indeed. Economical as always with his use of special angles to make the desired impact, Hitchcock's use of close-ups and low-angled shots is especially effective here and in the scene some days later when Bergman has become a virtual prisoner in the house. As the three of them are having coffee in the sitting room below, Hitchcock's ingenious editing conveys to us her sudden realization that she is being poisoned. When their visitor, Dr Anderson, goes to pick up her coffee cup by mistake, their simultaneous, quick reaction to correct him suddenly jolts her and she realizes for the first time why she feels so weak and helpless. But it is too late. She tries to leave, but collapses and is carried up to her bed. Hitchcock's use of close-ups of faces and objects – the key, the wine bottles, the cup of coffee – reflect the care with which the film has been put together.

Finally, the geography of the mansion is most fully exploited by Hitchcock in the neatly choreographed climactic sequence. Having realized that Bergman is being poisoned by Rains (and his mother), Grant arrives at the house, determined to rescue her. Seated in the main hallway, he suddenly sees the opportunity to dash up to her room on the first floor unobserved. In the dimly-lit bedroom, he puts his head on the pillow beside hers. It is a poignant, sensuous and moving moment as he kisses her and tries to reassure her that her ordeal is over and encourages her to summon up all her remaining strength to make it to the car he has waiting outside. (It is touching to see that, even in her weakened condition, she remembers her assignment and tries to tell him that she has learned of the location of the uranium deposits.)

As he helps her to descend the staircase, they are joined by the angry Rains and his mother, all four observed by Rains's Nazi friends below. Quick to size up the situation, and hoping to allay their suspicions, his mother tells Rains to act as if he and Grant are *both* taking her to the hospital. But Rains is then left behind to face an uncertain fate when the couple drive off.

Hitchcock clearly demonstrated his abilities as both producer and director here, not only responsible for the final cut but also for the film's subtle and restrained use of background music, in marked contrast to the Selznick style. The filming had gone smoothly, kept within budget and provided Hitch with his second smash hit in a row, but only two Oscar nominations – for Claude Rains's excellent performance as supporting actor, and for Ben Hecht's script.

It was ironic that, after six years under contract and already making plans to form his own, independent production company with British producer Sidney Bernstein, Hitchcock was suddenly faced with the prospect of collaborating really closely with Selznick for the first time. With *The Paradine Case* Hitchcock would fulfil the terms of his contract, and it would also be their last film together.

The Paradine Case was an old Selznick project that he had first become interested in when he was at MGM shortly after the book was published in 1933. The problems experienced by Alma Reville and James Bridie in adapting the old-fashioned story and bringing it up to date – it was now set in postwar London – led to Selznick deciding to write the final screenplay himself. However, the film would be filmed entirely in Hollywood, aside from some second unit footage of exteriors in London and Cumberland (in the Lake District), while the cast combined British actors, including Charles Laughton, Ann Todd, in her first American picture, and Leo G. Carroll, with Selznick's own contract stars: Alida Valli, as Mrs Paradine, Louis Jourdan and Gregory Peck. It was necessary to construct a number of elaborate interior sets. Most impressive (and expensive) of all was a detailed reconstruction of the Old Bailey courtroom where the long trial sequence takes place.

Selznick was still struggling to complete the screenplay when Hitchcock began shooting the film late in 1946, which meant that he was unable to plan out the production in his usual manner. It was based on a weak and poorly constructed story about a barrister who falls in love with the beautiful but mysterious widow whom he is meant to be defending against the charge of having murdered her husband. Unfortunately, not only was Gregory Peck miscast, but also his character is weakly developed. In the course of defending her, he attempts to implicate the valet (Louis Jourdan), while ignoring the circumstances of the murder itself, and never even asking her to give him her own version of what really happened.

We are meant to identify with him as he becomes increasingly involved in the case and infatuated with her, while his own marriage and relations with his sympathetic wife (Ann Todd) are put under great strain. If the film is meant to show the gradual decline and final humiliation of a brilliant young lawyer, it totally fails in this respect. For it is apparent from quite early on that he is not preparing the case properly, so that his dramatic courtroom admission of failure comes as no surprise at all. Gregory Peck tries hard, but appears extremely ill at ease in the role, especially in the courtroom sequences. This is made even more apparent by his un-English style of acting, contrasted with Charles Laughton as the wickedly precise and caustic judge, and the neat underplaying of Leo G. Carroll, one of Hitchcock's favourite character actors, as the prosecuting lawyer. Admittedly it is difficult to separate the weaknesses of Peck's performance from the incompetence of the character he is playing.

Unfortunately, these weaknesses are built into the structure of the film itself: the details of the crime are purposely neglected and never really explained properly, (their disclosure is saved for the courtroom sequences and to provide the build-up to the film's climax). Apparently, even Hitchcock was unsure of some of the details: 'I myself was never too clear as to how the murder was committed', he later admitted to François Truffaut, 'because it was complicated by people crossing from one room to another, up and down a corridor. I never truly understood the geography of that house or how she managed the killing.'

The excessively wordy script at least provided plenty of opportunities for the cast, and there was some fine acting in the film, most notably from Ann Todd; Laughton had some fun with the role of the lecherous old judge, and Ethel Barrymore was Oscar-nominated for her performance as his long-suffering wife, while Alida Valli is a chillingly sinister and alien presence at the core of the film, a kind of modern *femme fatale*, Joan Tetzel as a solicitor's daughter and Ann Todd's best friend provides a typically witty and outspoken commentary on the events in and out of the courtroom and serves as a link with the precocious American youngsters found in other Hitchcock films such as *Shadow of a Doubt* and *Strangers on a Train*. There are few other Hitchcock touches to appreciate in the film, but it does begin with a classic Hitchcock-style opening: The beautiful, but cold and sophisticated Mrs Paradine is seated at the piano in the drawing room of her luxurious home when the police suddenly arrive to arrest her, just before dinner. Hitchcock relishes showing us all the details of her humiliation as she is taken to Holloway Prison, charged, searched and locked up in a dark, gloomy cell. (He would develop this theme more fully in *The Wrong Man* ten years later.)

More Selznick than Hitchcock, as might be expected, a tremendous amount of time and effort went into this production. It is a well made film and reasonably successful at capturing the feel of the British settings (though with no hint of the shortages and rationing current in Britain at the time). But the many problems and delays in shooting meant that it went far over schedule and over budget – like all the other major Selznick productions from *Since You Went Away* (1944) to *Portrait of Jennie* (1948), with the notable exception of *Spellbound*. However, Selznick had found that through carefully planned and generously funded publicity campaigns, personally supervised by himself, he had been able to turn his long and expensive features into hits – most notably with *Since You Went Away* and *Duel in the Sun*. But he was unable to do so with *The Paradine Case*, released through his own new distribution company, the Selznick Releasing Organization (SRO). For movie audiences were changing, they were less easily influenced by his well orchestrated publicity and had already declined substantially from their wartime peak. Ninety-two days in production, *The Paradine Case* had cost $4 million, more than twice as much as *Spellbound*, and, if inflation is taken into account, rates as the most expensive film of Hitchcock's entire career.

To a certain extent, this pattern of relatively small productions growing longer, broader in scope and ever more expensive, reflected Selznick's insecurity and loss of confidence in his own abilities as a producer, his determination to get everything exactly right, no matter what the cost, and his reluctance to release his films before they had been seen repeatedly by preview audiences and re-worked or re-edited to his satisfaction. At the same time this loss of confidence reflected problems in his personal life, the gradual decline of his company, which had been losing many of its top stars and technical personnel, and especially, his inability to put his memories of *Gone with the Wind* behind him. This was seen most clearly in the case of *Duel in the Sun*, transformed in the course of production from a moderate-size Western into a full blown epic, his most lavish production of the 1940s. (At well over $5 million, it actually cost more than *Gone with the Wind*.) Similarly, his obsession was apparent on a smaller, black-and-white picture like *The Paradine Case*. According to Selznick biographer Bob Thomas, Gregory Peck discovered him in his office one day, immersed in plans to make the film substantially broader in scope. 'My God, David, aren't you going overboard on the grandeur of this little drama in Old Bailey?' he asked. To which David replied, 'I'll tell you why. Because I've got to do better than *Gone with the Wind*. I may never make it. But I've got to try.'

The first signs of a changed Selznick had already been evident as early as 1939, the year of his greatest triumph. Suffering from severe overwork and having driven himself relentlessly for a number of years, he decided to close down his studio temporarily. Already in September of that year he had negotiated his first, fairly profitable deal to loan out Hitchcock's services to Walter Wanger for *Foreign Correspondent*. During the following years he became a packager, a deal maker and an agent all rolled into one. As his wife, Irene, unhappy at the time, later recalled, 'To keep up his spirits, he resorted to momentum. He signed actors he didn't need. He registered titles and used them for trading purposes. Talent commitments and remake rights turned into irresistible commodities. He became devoted to negotiations . . . He made such good deals it became an insidious habit. He did everything but make a picture.' For Hitchcock, in particular, there were obvious benefits; the various loan-outs gave him the opportunity to work for a large number of different producers and studios under a variety of conditions, and he generally functioned more freely than if he had been forced to make his films for the meticulous and demanding Selznick alone.

Having given up producing for a time, it had then been difficult for Selznick to get started again. Though only in his mid-forties, and a few years younger than Hitchcock, he had already outlived his time. Nominally known as an independent producer, he was really a product of the studio system where the producer was boss and writers, directors and stars were all employees under contract. Although he occasionally took a chance on a film 'original', like the big studios, he most often took the

In the dramatic final confrontation of *Rope* (1948), James Stewart returns to accuse the two young murderers, his former students, in the living room of their New York apartment. This was the first of Stewart's four films with Hitch, while Farley Granger (left) would also star in Hitchcock's *Strangers on a Train* (1951). Hitch had originally hoped to cast Montgomery Clift as the more dominant and psychopathic of the two young men, but this role was eventually filled by John Dall (right).

'great novels' approach to film-making – you buy the rights to a success-ful book or play, then hire writers and a director to turn it into a film with the emphasis on stars and production values. As one writer noted, 'Selznick's tastes were remarkably consistent with those of the classical Hollywood; his concept of prestige film-making was shaped during the studio era, and his sense of dramatic qualities and production values, and of marketing and exhibition practices, had been very much in line with the industry's' (Schatz).

In addition, Selznick refused to recognize the fact that in the 1940s the creative balance was shifting more in favour of the director at the expense of the producer, and that audiences, too, were changing and could more readily accept adult themes characterized by a sophisticated or subtle treatment. More at ease with words than with images, Selznick's films of the mid-1940s seem overly wordy and literary and, especially, over-produced, most often running two hours or longer. With regard to the three Hitchcocks, his approach could still prove effective on a film such as *Spellbound*, but could equally well turn out badly, as with *The Paradine Case*. And neither could compare with *Notorious*, the product of a creative cinematic mind, conceived and made as a film, not a production package, with Hitchcock, not Selznick, as producer and director.

Able to make favourable deals with the major studios, the leading directors were no longer willing to put up with Selznick's behaviour. If anything, he had become *more* unpredictable and dictatorial over the years and allowed his directors even less creative freedom. On *Duel in the Sun*, for example, in Selznick's own words, '. . . there were strict orders on the set that not a single scene was to be photographed . . . until I was telephoned to come down on the set to check the lighting, the setup, and the rehearsal. Day after day, setup after setup.' But Selznick suffered a serious blow to his reputation when director King Vidor walked off the film in the middle of production.

Eight years after he had first arrived in Hollywood, Hitchcock was still the only director on long-term contract to Selznick. Once he had completed *The Paradine Case* he had fulfilled the terms of his contract and refused to sign with Selznick again. His next films would be made for his own production company, Transatlantic Pictures, a British-American company set up by him in partnership with British producer Sidney Bernstein.

In his book *Hitchcock and Selznick*, Leonard Leff discusses the creative partnership between the two men with special emphasis on what he sees as Selznick's influence on Hitchcock, this need to 'control' Hitchcock's excesses, and the director's dependence on the producer. But it appears quite obvious that Leff grossly overstates his arguments, even going so far as to dismiss most of Hitchcock's non-Selznick films from *Foreign Correspondent* to *Rope* and *Dial M for Murder*, and is incredibly disparaging of his early films, referred to as 'the fairy tale melodrama of his British period.' ('In the late 1930s, Selznick had rescued Hitchcock from drowning in the tempestuous waters of British film production.')

In addition, Leff attempts to credit *Notorious*, the best Hitchcock film of the mid-1940s, as a Selznick production, though this is clearly stretching the truth. In a practical sense, Selznick's most active contribution to their first two films together, *Rebecca* and *Spellbound*, took place in post-production. On *Notorious*, Hitchcock handled this himself.

Comparison of costs and rentals of Hitchcock's two biggest 1940s hits ($)

SPELLBOUND	(1944–45)	NOTORIOUS	(1945–46)
$150,000	Hitchcock (director)	$339,000	Hitchcock (director & producer)
40,000	rights to novel	–	
70,000	Ben Hecht/script	61,000	Ben Hecht/script
220,000	Ingrid Bergman ($17,500 per wk × 12.5 wks)	200,000	Ingrid Bergman
33,850	Gregory Peck ($3,125 per wk × 11 wks)	550,000	Cary Grant
50,000	Selznick (producer)	–	
563,850	Main above-the-line costs (director/producer/script/stars)	1,150,000	Above-the-line costs
1,107,000	Other costs	1,225,000	Other costs
1,670,000	TOTAL COSTS	2,375,000	TOTAL COSTS
$7 m	Box office gross	$8 m	Box office gross
4,700,000	(USA & Canada) rentals	4,800,000	(USA & Canada) rentals
		1,700,000	Overseas rentals
		6,500,000	Total rentals revenue
		4,500,000	Expenses
		2,000,000	Profits: divided equally between RKO and Selznick (1 million each)

The total box office gross is divided among exhibitors, distributor and producer, i.e., the rentals figure (with the exhibitor cut deducted) is set against the total expenses to determine the final profit. Unfortunately, complete information is not available for *Spellbound* which was, nevertheless, only slightly less profitable than *Notorious*.

Of course, Selznick made pre-production contributions – suggestions on the script, casting, etc. – but this hardly makes *Notorious* a Selznick film. In fact, it is remarkable how little time the two men actually spent working together until *The Paradine Case*, the last and least of their collaborations. All in all, not much of a partnership, and the direct influence of Selznick on Hitchcock is not all that apparent, either.

On the other hand, a much stronger case could be made for the influence of Ben Hecht on Hitchcock, though Leff hardly even hints at this possibility. They collaborated closely over a period of many months on the scripts for both *Spellbound* and *Notorious*, both highly successful pictures. The two men got on well from the start. Hecht concentrated on dialogue and storyline, while Hitchcock provided a strong visual sense and an eye for detail, and 'gave off plot turns like a Roman candle', as Hecht himself later recalled. The partnership proved even more effective on *Notorious*, and an amusing description of one of their story conferences was even published at the time:

> Mr Hecht would stride about or drape himself over chair or couch, or sprawl artistically on the floor. Mr Hitchcock, a 192–pound Buddha (reduced from 295) would sit primly on a straight-back chair, his hands clasped across his midriff, his round button eyes gleaming. They would talk from nine to six; Mr Hecht would sneak off with his typewriter for two or three days; then they would have another conference. The dove of peace lost not a pinfeather in the process. They did not even play jokes on each other.

Not only did they work well together, but also Hitch became more clearly aware than ever before of the best kind of writing collaboration that he could expect in Hollywood. The partnership with Hecht would serve as a model for Hitchcock's work with his writers in the future and especially during the highly productive 1950s.

5

1948-53: Hitchcock Goes Independent

From *Rope* to *Dial M for Murder*

I. 1948–49: Transatlantic

Hitchcock was but one of the many leading Hollywood directors who set up their own independent production companies during the postwar years. Late in 1945, for example, Frank Capra, George Stevens and William Wyler had joined together to form Liberty Films. At Enterprise Studios, set up in 1946, the leading names were Lewis Milestone, Robert Rossen, and writer-director Abraham Polonsky, while John Ford founded Argosy Productions with producer Merian C. Cooper later in 1946 around the same time that Hitchcock was finalizing his partnership with Sidney Bernstein in Transatlantic Pictures.

By this time, Hitchcock was very much a part of the Hollywood scene, and he played a key role in the changes taking place. Whereas most other small companies had distribution arrangements with RKO or United Artists, the two obvious choices, Hitchcock was able to make a special deal with Warner Bros. As Thomas Schatz has pointed out, 'an important precedent was set when Warners agreed to serve as distributor for Transatlantic', marking a major step for the studio away from producing all its own pictures, as the studio era was gradually coming to an end.

Although Selznick was still hoping , up to the very end, that Hitchcock would eventually agree to sign a new contract with him after the shooting of *The Paradine Case* was completed, Hitch immediately began work on the first treatment of his first Transatlantic picture, *Rope*. He collaborated initially with Hume Cronyn, then brought in the young playwright Arthur Laurents to do the final script and dialogue, though he also made use of dialogue from the original play by Patrick Hamilton. He recognized here, in this stage thriller with all the action confined to a single room on one day, an ideal subject for him to extend further his previous attempts at pre-planning his films as he had on *Notorious* and especially *Lifeboat*, with its similar confinement to a single setting.

The idea was to shoot the entire film in sequence, in the studio, making use of extremely long takes. In fact, the individual shots were so long that this required extensive rehearsing with the cast and crew, with many unusual technical problems to solve. At the time it was first released (and ever since), *Rope* has been widely written about as the first feature filmed entirely in 10-minute long takes, with each shot lasting for the full length of the roll of film in the camera. However, as Robin Wood has pointed out, there are *no* 10-minute takes. There are a total of eleven shots in the film, mostly varying in length from five to eight minutes, with a three-minute take for the opening and credits, and just three shots lasting over nine minutes.

In addition, the idea of filming a play with long takes suggests that the camera would generally view the action from a distance, with an emphasis on medium long or long shots, but with some camera mobility that would allow the actors to play out their roles a bit as they would on the stage. This was the kind of technique used to shoot some of the early talkies adapted from plays. They looked like filmed theatre, with the camera partly immobilized by its soundproof box and the actors' movements restricted by the placing of the microphone. However, as one of the most visually aware directors, Hitchcock would never shoot a film in this way.

He himself has referred to the film as 'precut', and it is remarkable how closely it resembles the pattern of normal film editing practice. But instead of the moving camera shots being followed by a close-up or a long shot, the camera achieves this effect within the same unbroken take, i.e., it moves in to a close-up of a face or some object, then pulls back to take in the entire room. The only difference here is one of time – it takes a bit longer for the camera to make its moves, and one is occasionally aware of a laboured and unnecessary camera movement. As Ray Durgnat has noted, 'on a storyboard, the film would read as a conventional affair of close-ups, two-shots and deep focus groupings.' Similarly, as described by Gene Phillips, the camera 'unobtrusively glides from one group of characters to another, closing in at times to capture a key gesture or remark, then falling back for a medium or long shot as the action and dialogue continue. By using a total of 150 different camera movements to achieve the equivalent number of individual shots, Hitchcock was "cutting the film inside the camera" to achieve the same effect as if he had actually photographed 150 separate shots and then spliced them together.'

Furthermore, this technique has the effect of bringing the apartment remarkably to life, almost like another character in the film. And we gain a special familiarity with the setting, which contributes immeasurably to our involvement with the events taking place there.

Since the film begins with a particularly brutal looking murder (by strangling), which we know will be uncovered by the end, the movie audience becomes involved in a special kind of way – we, along with the two young murderers become witnesses in a kind of grisly charade. The other characters who arrive for a dinner party, among them the dead boy's father, aunt and girl friend, are unaware that his dead body is hidden in the large chest that sits prominently in the living room of the apartment. There are various clues dropped during the course of the evening, and it is left to the young men's college teacher (James Stewart) to discover the horrible truth. Full of black humour of a type that Hitch was to exploit to more comical effect in *The Trouble with Harry* seven years later, the film's development is dependent on lots of little details: the stuttering of one of the boys when he gets excited, a broken glass and bleeding hand, the murdered boy's hat and the murder weapon, the short length of rope that reappears at various points.

The performances of John Dall and Farley Granger in the difficult roles of the young murderers – loosely based on the real life Leopold and Loeb case – were more than adequate, while James Stewart is especially good in an unusual and downbeat role for him. This was the first of his four films for Hitchcock; their second, *Rear Window*, would similarly take place entirely within a New York apartment and involve him in the solving of a murder. In *Rope*, Hitchcock was making use of a largely American cast for the first time since *Lifeboat* and *Shadow of a Doubt* five years earlier; it is his most American film of the middle and late 1940s, though he does use the occasional American star in his otherwise British films (Gregory Peck in *The Paradine Case*, Joseph Cotten in *Under Capricorn* and Jane Wyman in *Stage Fright*).

Aside from a few weak bits – Stewart is required to make a particularly long and awkward speech near the end about how his teachings have been perverted and twisted by his two students – *Rope* works extremely well as a film and is notable not only for its long takes and its sensitive treatment of a difficult subject, but also for its effective use of sound, with virtually no background music. (One of the characters plays the piano.) In addition, this was Hitchcock's first film in colour in which he seems to be following his own comments of ten years earlier when he had written: 'I should never want to fill the screen with colour: it ought to be used economically . . .'

So much attention has been paid to Hitch's use of long takes that the colour theme has been neglected by most critics writing about the film,

and none of them appear to be aware of its special significance, representing a particularly interesting aspect of Hitchcock's qualities as an
innovator. The use of colour here suggests that Hitchcock wished to
avoid the typical low-keyed approach of forties *film noir* in keeping with
the central theme – that most of the characters are unaware that anything out of the ordinary has happened – the apartment has a normal,
everyday, upper middle-class look to it. Most importantly, the colour is
also useful in telescoping the time period covered and in making the
transition from late afternoon to evening. (As Chabrol and Rohmer have
pointed out, 'thanks above all to the use of colour, we pass imphercepti-
bely from the sunny afternoon of the murder to the night of the last few
minutes.')

Unfortunately, the colour of the sunset effect came out too orangey
and required some reshooting, according to Hitchcock. But otherwise
filming in colour presented him with no additional technical problems.
Though the slowness of colour stock required additional lighting, the
Technicolor camera was not significantly larger or more bulky than the
Mitchell currently in use for most black-and-white filming in Hollywood
at the time. An important bonus in filming the long takes in colour was
that it was then possible to simplify much of the lighting. As Hitch
himself pointed out, 'I especially admired the approach to lighting used
by the Americans . . . because it overcame the two-dimensional nature of
the image by separating the actor from the background through the use
of backlights . . . to detach him from his setting. Now in colour there is
no need for this . . .'

Of special significance here is the fact that, as late as 1948, Hitchcock
was still one of the first of the top Hollywood directors to film in
Technicolor and the first to shoot a thriller in colour. (Perhaps the closest
to a colour thriller prior to *Rope* was Paramount's relatively cheaply
made horror-adventure drama set in the South American jungle, *Dr
Cyclops* (1940), while later in the 1940s there were two other 'crime
dramas' filmed in Technicolor – *Leave Her to Heaven* (1945) and *Desert
Fury* (1947).) Although the first three-strip Technicolor feature had been
filmed in 1935, by the mid-1940s, ten years later, only 10 per cent of
Hollywood features from the major studios were being filmed in colour
and these were predominantly musicals with a few Westerns and costume pictures. (Among those leading directors who did not make their
first colour feature until the 1950s were Capra, Cukor, Huston, Kazan,
Mankiewicz, Mann, Ray, Sirk, Wise, Stevens, Wyler and Zinnemann.)
Not only was filming in colour more expensive, but also there were
strong preconceptions regarding what types of films were most suitable,
with a definite bias against using colour in dramatic pictures. The

conventional view, hardly challenged at the time by leading American directors, was that colour would distract the audience and detract from the drama. Crime or thriller movies were especially closely identified with black-and-white up to the 1960s. Thus Hitchcock's regular use of colour in his pictures from 1953 on would set him apart from other directors of this type of film. His preference for colour can be seen as but one additional aspect of his efforts to upgrade the suspense movie genre, related to his use of top stars and technicians and a preference for mainstream budgets, too.

Having used colour for the first time in *Rope*, Hitchcock obviously felt he was ready to try something a bit more ambitious with his next film. It was a special coup for him, as producer, to succeed in signing Ingrid Bergman, his favourite female star, who was tremendously in demand at the time. *Under Capricorn* was specially designed for her and planned as Hitch's first film in England and his first costume picture for ten years, since *Jamaica Inn*, in fact. Possibly he was aware that the beautiful Miss Bergman had not yet appeared on the screen in a stylish costume picture in colour. *Under Capricorn* would, in a sense, turn out to be her only Technicolor costumer of the 1940s. (Both of her other early Technicolor movies, *For Whom the Bell Tolls* (1943) and *Joan of Arc* (1948) presented a 'deglamourized' Bergman on the screen, using little make-up and wearing only simple, plain-looking or men's clothes.)

Although the project was obviously set up with one eye on the box office, and the substantial fee to Bergman reflected her current status as a top drawing star, this was a strange and risky venture for Hitchcock and his new company at a time when movie attendances were declining. Even before filming began, in the summer of 1948, Bergman's box-office appeal had been brought into question by the failure of *Arch of Triumph*, co-starring Charles Boyer.

Having broken with Selznick, Hitchcock was here, surprisingly, returning to the kind of romantic melodrama that was a Selznick speciality and did not readily lend itself to the 'Hitchcock touch'. In fact, the film appears as a virtual summation of his Selznick years from *Rebecca* to *The Paradine Case*; insecure and unhappy, the heroine is dominated by a shrewish housekeeper, and relations between her and her rich husband are clouded by some dark event in their past (*Rebecca*); she is a bit of an alcoholic, and a virtual prisoner in her own house, and is possibly being poisoned, too (*Notorious*); while the 'lady and the groom' theme and her involvement in an unsolved killing echo *The Paradine Case*.

Though she looks lovely in colour, Ingrid Bergman was obviously miscast as the aristocratic Lady Henrietta, as was Joseph Cotten playing Flusky, her husband, formerly her Irish groom who has become a

successful businessman in Australia having served a ten-year sentence for a murder he did not commit. The first half of the film is by far the best. We identify with the young arrival, Michael Wilding, introduced to the various characters and to the Flusky mansion by some adroit camerawork, leading up to the first striking appearance of Bergman, barefoot and looking very pale and dishevelled and drunk, twenty minutes into the film. The turning point in the plot comes about midway through the picture with her rehabilitation and her triumphant and radiant appearance at the governor's ball. Her transformation is made even more striking by the glowing Technicolor photography and the stylish period costumes designed by Roger Furse.

But from this point on the film deteriorates badly. Violent confrontations – Cotten versus the governor, Cotten fighting with, and shooting, Wilding – alternate with equally melodramatic revelations – Bergman, rather than Cotten, had shot her brother years ago, while the housekeeper is in love with Cotten and has been scheming to get rid of Bergman. Whereas we had earlier been led to identify with Wilding, he later becomes a marginal figure. The picture's unsatisfactory plot structure is especially apparent near the end when he departs from Australia, as he had arrived, but leaving the now happily reconciled couple behind.

An overly wordy, studio-bound production, Hitchcock again made use of long takes that allowed the actors the opportunity to deliver some lengthy speeches and helped to convey an excellent feel for the Flusky mansion setting. In fact, there are relatively few exterior scenes, and it hardly seems to matter that the story is set in Australia, for we see very little of the country and leading characters are either Irish or English.

Though nicely subdued and tasteful in its use of colour, the Technicolor filming helped push the cost of the picture up to $2\frac{1}{2}$ million, substantially more than *Rope*, which had itself cost more than Hitchcock had originally expected. (The use of long takes was meant to speed up filming and cut costs.) But it did less well at the box office, too. Whereas *Rope* had made a small profit, *Under Capricorn* recorded a substantial loss and thus marked the virtual end of Transatlantic Pictures and of Hitchcock's 1940s experiments in colour filming. (He would carry on as a

A candid shot catches Hitch in action while filming *Under Capricorn* in 1948. (Star Michael Wilding can be glimpsed in the background.) This was the second of his two films for his own independent production company, Transatlantic Pictures, and the first time that he had returned to Britain to direct a feature since his departure for Hollywood in 1939.

relatively independent producer-director making his pictures in black-and-white for Warner Bros for the next four years before returning to colour (and 3-D) with *Dial M for Murder* in 1953.) For Bergman this was her third high cost flop in a row; possibly she set some sort of record as, within the space of two years, each had led to the demise of a fledging independent company. In fact, *Under Capricorn* was by far the least expensive, and probably suffered the smallest losses, of the three. (The box office failure of *Arch of Triumph*, cost $4¼ million, and *Joan of Arc*, at $5 million, marked the end for both Enterpise and Walter Wanger's Sierra Pictures, respectively – undoubtedly contributing to Bergman's decision to make a break with Hollywood and go off to Italy to make films with leading Italian director Roberto Rossellini.)

Just as Hitchcock had joined the trend of leading directors forming their own independent companies after the war, similarly he was in good company a few years later with the failure of Transatlantic, around the same time as Enterprise and following the demise of Liberty. And just as directors Frank Capra, William Wyler and George Stevens would find themselves as producer-directors with somewhat less creative control, making their pictures at Paramount for a few years, similarly Hitchcock would spend the next five years at Warner Bros. Clearly, it had always been difficult for small, independent companies making quality pictures to survive in Hollywood, a lesson which Selznick, for one, had learned many years before. (His supposedly successful production company had recorded small losses for many years before the release of *Gone with the Wind* brought sudden and spectacular profits.)

II. 1949–53: Warner Bros

Perhaps eager to put the failure of *Under Capricorn* behind him, Hitchcock lost no time in selecting the book (*Man Running* by Selwyn Jepson) that he planned to adapt for the screen as the first film in his new, four-picture deal with Warner Bros, a deal that allowed him a really remarkable degree of freedom in his choice of subject, cast and writers. By the end of 1948 he and his wife, Alma, were hard at work with playwright Whitfield Cook on the script of the new film, which would be retitled *Stage Fright*.

A lightweight British thriller in the style that Hitchcock himself made popular in the late 1930s, the film opens with a murder and with Richard Todd as the leading suspect on the run from the police. The main suspense of the plot hinges on the question of whether Marlene Dietrich's husband was killed by Todd or whether she killed him herself, as

Todd alleges and that he merely helped her to get rid of the evidence. Unfortunately, the great disparity in ages and acting styles between Todd and Dietrich contributes to a totally unconvincing relationship on screen that is not helped by a weak script and story line. It is difficult to believe that they are actually lovers. In addition the 35-year-old Jane Wyman is implausibly cast as a young RADA student to whom Todd turns for help – an obvious echo here of Hitchcock's earlier, and better, British film *Young and Innocent* (1937). Not only are Todd and Wyman rather dull, as well as miscast, but the film also lacks tension and there is no real 'villain'. Todd who is finally revealed as the murderer, is himself quite disturbed and afraid, while, as Truffaut points out, 'none of the people . . . are ever in real danger'. Dietrich plays a larger than life version of herself, which she does quite well. She appears to have strayed in from another film, but an undoubted bonus is the opportunity to see her singing and performing on stage.

Reflecting Hitch's interest in varying his films, *Stage Fright* is quite different from his other forties productions, though slightly related to *Saboteur* with its man on the run theme, which was itself derived from his earlier British thrillers. Though the film includes a number of typically Hitchcockian touches and memorable comic cameos from Miles Malleson, Joyce Grenfell and especially Alistair Sim as Jane Wyman's father (!), the plot becomes increasingly weak and complicated in the second half and lacks a convincing climax. As Hitchcock himself explained to Truffaut, 'The book had just come out and several of the reviewers had mentioned that it might make a good Hitchcock picture. And I, like an idiot, believed them.'

Having lost his own company Hitchcock was now back in a similar position to that which he had enjoyed with the Selznick loanouts a few years earlier – able to function as a producer-director with a fair degree of creative freedom, but without the responsibility of financing the films himself through his own production company. But whereas the Selznick years had led to such pictures as *Foreign Correspondent*, *Shadow of a Doubt* and *Notorious*, among others, he appears to have temporarily lost his special touch during this later period. A poor choice of subjects was compounded by some serious weaknesses in casting.

In fairness to Hitchcock one must bear in mind that this was a particularly unsettled period in the development of the American cinema. The big studios were experiencing major problems as they changed over from a contract system that had operated effectively for over 20 years, while at the same time they were being forced to sell off their film theatres. Attendances continued to decline from the peak levels seen in the war years.

John Russell Taylor, Hitchcock's official biographer, refers to the late 1940s as 'a strange period of dissatisfaction and lack of direction for him' when he also suffered from hypochondria and was 'subject to all kinds of minor ailments, probably of a nervous or psychosomatic origin'. Yet this lack of cinematic inspiration continued well into the 1950s. Although he did make a comeback at the box office, enjoying a modest commercial success with his last three Warner Bros productions, *Strangers on a Train* was the only outstanding film of this period and it did not really provide him with the new sense of direction he needed.

During these years he had set himself various creative challenges, had embarked on *Under Capricorn* especially for Ingrid Bergman, tried his hand at a comedy thriller (*Stage Fright*) and turned to an old project dating back to the 1930s (*I Confess*) since he had trouble finding new material that appealed to him. *Dial M for Murder* was a conventional, if stylish, adaptation of a stage thriller in which any creative input was hampered by having to shoot the film in 3-D. Yet an important aspect of Hitchcock's problems was his apparent difficulty in finding suitable subjects. The failure of *Stage Fright*, for example, demonstrated the risk of merely falling back on old, familiar formulas.

Hitchcock's next film *Strangers on a Train*, however, was an unusual and modern type of psychological thriller, notable for its treatment of the characters within a classic Hitchcockian blend of serious themes with his much favoured ironic qualities and black humour. This picture was really a bit special. Whereas all of Hitch's best films after he'd gone to the US were either based on a strong original story (*Rebecca, Psycho*), emerged from close collaboration with a leading writer (*Shadow of a Doubt, Notorious, North by Northwest*) or an effective combination of the two (*Rear Window, The Wrong Man, Vertigo, The Birds*), *Strangers on a Train* does not fit into any of these categories. The original book is a weak first novel from the then young, aspiring thriller writer Patricia Highsmith. But Hitchcock could clearly see its potential as the starting point for an effective and original film.

Unfortunately, Hitchcock was unsuccessful in his attempts to find a leading crime writer to collaborate with him on the script. His first choice, Dashiell Hammett, fell through, while Raymond Chandler proved unsuitable. However, Chandler's well documented complaints regarding his work on the script provide a fascinating clue to the true nature of the project. Although Hitchcock always preferred to plan out his films well in advance and work closely with his writers, in this case he appears to have had an especially strong sense of the cinematic potential of the original story and a clear image in his mind of how the film should take shape, rejecting anything that did not fit in with this vision. Thus, he really needed a writer who was willing to submit to his conception and be satisfied merely to assist him in filling in the details and dialogue and generally help to give substance to his story ideas. This Chandler was unable or unwilling to do. As he wrote to his British publisher, Hamish Hamilton, 'The thing that amuses me about Hitchcock is the way he directs a film in his head before he knows what the story is'. And to his agent, Ray Stark, he complained that Hitchcock was 'full of little suggestions and ideas which have a cramping effect on a writer's initiative.' Hitchcock, too, later recalled that their collaboration had not gone well at all, that Chandler had reacted to some of his ideas by asserting, 'If you can go it alone, why the hell do you need me?' But when Hitchcock left him on his own, Chandler complained about a lack of contact with the director. His second draft of the screenplay was even less satisfactory to Hitchcock who then decided to look for a writer elsewhere. According to Chandler, when he saw the final script he found that Hitchcock had 'succeeded in removing almost every trace of my writing from it'. In fact, Hitchcock had succeeded in getting what he needed from one of Ben Hecht's script assistants, Czenzi Ormonde, with contributions from Hecht, Barbara Keon and his wife, Alma Hitchcock, only a week or two before he was due to begin shooting.

The completed film serves as a virtual archetype of screen adaptation. The basic idea of the book, of an 'exchange of murders', is ingenious but the original novel is diffuse and fails to sustain its main thriller theme. It covers a period of about $1\frac{1}{2}$ years and jumps about the US from the East Coast (New York, Long Island) to Texas and even Mexico. Hitchcock has concentrated the material quite remarkably and it benefits from this and a momentum that carries the viewer along. Cutting out much of the superfluous material, and making use of a much shorter time span of a few summer months, he has made many important changes while stressing the relationship between the two men at the core of the story.

His sense of American geography was also well served as the film gains from being confined to the mid-Atlantic corridor extending from New York to Washington, DC, from the upper class milieu of Long Island and tennis at Forest Hills, to Washington, with its national monuments and political associations, and the small town of Metcalf, a relatively short journey from New York, located between them. This was Hitch's very first 'East Coast' movie, though he would make effective use of Eastern settings in a number of his later films, such as *The Trouble with Harry* (set in New England), *The Wrong Man* (New York City), the opening reels of *North by Northwest* and *Marnie* (Philadelphia, Baltimore). This was, in fact, his first really American film since *Shadow of a Doubt* eight years earlier and it demonstrates how brilliantly he could respond to real American settings, effectively blended with more stylized studio interiors.

Hitchcock retained the best bits of the novel, especially the opening meeting on the train and the fairground murder, but hardly made use of the rest of the book at all. The most serious flaw in the novel – having murdered Guy's wife, Bruno succeeds in pressuring Guy into killing his father – is given a new and more plausible twist in the film. He was also fortunate in his casting. Robert Walker is brilliant making the quirkily malevolent role of Bruno his own – undoubtedly the most memorable performance of his short career. (He died after acting in only one more film.) Unable to get William Holden for the other leading part, Hitchcock settled for Farley Granger who portrayed Guy as a somewhat weaker and more vulnerable character. Rather than there being a clear contrast between the idle, pleasure-seeking and degenerate Bruno and the successful young architect Guy found in the novel, in the film the characters obviously have much more in common. Both of them appear quite well off, though neither has a real job or profession. Guy is a leading amateur tennis player who has ideas of dabbling in politics and looks forward to gaining an easy entrée into that world through his fiancée, a senator's daughter, while his relationship with the mentally unstable Bruno brings out his own insecurities and neuroses. Guy in the film appears more ambivalent in his relations with Bruno, both attracted and repelled by him and thus more convincingly involved in Bruno's ingenious and sinister plotting. (Granger's performance inevitably recalls his role in *Rope* in which he played the more sensitive and easily influenced of the two young murderers, dominated by the more outspoken and confident character played by John Dall, not too different from his relationship with Walker here.)

After their initial meeting on the train, unlike in the book there are relatively few additional scenes between Guy and Bruno, in keeping with Bruno's 'exchange of murders' idea, that they must remain 'strangers' and never meet openly if the plot is to work. From this point on, though their lives are intertwined, they are generally observed separately as Hitchcock makes use of a parallel structure leading up to the famous crosscutting sequence, superbly paced and edited, near the end of the film: Guy increases the pace and changes from his normal style of play as he strains to win an important tennis match as quickly as possible, knowing that Bruno is just then on his way to plant Guy's cigarette lighter as an important piece of incriminating evidence at the spot where Guy's wife was murdered. The brightly lit action on the tennis court is contrasted with Bruno's progress and especially the tension of his efforts to retrieve the lighter when it accidentally falls down

Robert Walker (right) is deadly serious as he outlines his ingenious idea of an 'exchange of murders' to Farley Granger who thinks he must be joking and tries to laugh it off – an early scene from *Strangers on a Train* (1951). In a radical departure from his previous roles, Walker emerged as one of the most memorable of Hitchcock villains, while Hitch himself received the first of his three awards from the Directors Guild of America for his work on this gripping and memorable thriller.

inside a sewer grating. This sequence, in turn, leads to the final, gripping climax as Guy catches up with Bruno and the two men are locked in a fierce struggle on a fairground merry-go-round as it goes crazily out of control.

Hitchcock was well served by other members of his cast too: Laura Elliott as Guy's nasty and vindictive estranged wife, Marian – quite attractive behind her ugly, thick glasses, which fall to the ground as she is attacked by Bruno (we observe the murder, distorted and reflected in the giant lens); Marion Lorne is excellent as Bruno's batty, indulgent mother who has no idea what is going on, and Patricia Hitchcock plays the precocious younger sister of Guy's fiancée, quite amusingly outspoken and knowledgeable about police procedure. She too wears glasses and bears a slight resemblance to Marian; thus, in one of the film's most memorable sequences, Bruno is suddenly mesmerized by the sight of her face as he is jokingly demonstrating how to strangle an elderly lady at a swank party. Obviously reliving the earlier murder, he goes into a kind of trance and has to be violently subdued. The only serious weakness in the casting is that of Ruth Roman who appears a bit dull and unconvincing as Guy's fiancée, Anne. Since she was a contract star at Warner Bros at this time, Hitchcock was forced to use her, against his better judgment.

Characteristic of Hitchcock at his best, the film is full of telling little details: the incriminating lighter, a gift from Anne, with its inscription 'From A to G' and crossed tennis racquets motif; the quite compellingly original tracking shots at the opening of the film, following the progress of two pairs of feet arriving at Washington's Union Station and boarding the northbound train, and two sets of converging railway lines leading up to the first meeting between Guy and Bruno; Bruno innocently eating popcorn as he stalks his prey at the fairground – when menaced by a little boy with a gun, he reacts by bursting the child's balloon with a cigarette; the reaction of a little old lady in the back seat when two detectives chasing Guy jump into her limousine – 'We're chasing a man' to which she responds, 'How very exciting.'

Strangers on a Train marked an important return to form for Hitchcock after the problems of the late 1940s, and of special interest is the fact that the revival of his career was closely linked to his return to mainstream Hollywood. All of his fifties pictures were produced through a few top studios – Warner Bros, then Paramount, with one MGM production of note (*North by Northwest*), and made use of leading Hollywood stars, writers and technicians even on those few films shot partly in Canada (*I Confess*) or abroad (*To Catch a Thief, The Man Who Knew Too Much*). Yet Hitchcock still resisted the temptation to become more 'Americanized', and, in spite of the success of the most 'American' of his films, he appears to have been strangely slow to recognize and take advantage of this fact. (If one compiled a list of his best films during 1939–54, for example, it would be headed by *Shadow of a Doubt, Notorious, Strangers on a Train* and *Rear Window*, three out of four very American, with American stars and settings.)

As he arrives at the town of Metcalf, tennis champ Farley Granger passes the familiar, bulky figure of Alfred Hitchcock about to board the train carrying a large double bass. Well known for his cameo appearances over the years, these were often used by Hitch – as here, in *Strangers on a Train* – as a means of injecting a bit of tongue-in-cheek humour into his films.

The success of *Strangers on a Train* did not do much to revive his career, for he was still having difficulties finding suitable projects during the early and mid-1950s and continued to alternate American with British or foreign subjects. In fact, there was a long and unprecedented gap of almost two years between the filming of *Strangers on a Train* in the autumn of 1950 and *I Confess*, filmed in the late summer and autumn of 1952, which meant that there was no Hitchcock film released in 1952 – the first time that he had missed out a year since the very beginnings of his career as a director in 1926.

I Confess was based on a play, *Nos Deux Consciences* by Paul Anthelme, which had first interested him in the 1930s, and for which he had bought the rights in the 1940s. Hitchcock had never filmed in Canada before, but now took his American crew and stars to Quebec, which he rightly saw as the nearest and most convenient equivalent to the French Catholic origins of the play. The main theme appealed to Hitchcock, who was himself a Catholic, as it concerned a priest who hears the confession of a murderer but is bound by the secrecy of the confessional and is unable to clear himself when he is accused of the crime. In Hitchcock's hands the film emerged as yet another variation on the familiar (Hitchcockian) theme of the 'wrongly accused man'. It is closely related to his later (and better) picture set in New York and starring Henry Fonda, *The Wrong Man* (1956).

Although Hitchcock later claimed that film audiences at the time had found it difficult to accept that a priest would remain silent under such circumstances, the picture was reasonably successful at the box office, reflecting the current popularity of its star, Montgomery Clift. In fact, the film suffers from other, more serious weaknesses. The plot is contrived in such a way as to provide a substantial body of circumstantial evidence implicating the priest in the crime. For example, it turns out that the dead man had been blackmailing the priest's former girlfriend, who is now married, and they are seen together at the scene of the crime, for they just happen to have planned to confront the blackmailer that very morning when his body is discovered. In addition, a priest had been seen leaving the house where the murder took place, and Clift has no alibi for the time of the murder. This means that there is an additional explanation for the priest's continuing silence and no need for film audiences to accept, or be familiar with, the absolute secrecy of the confessional. Even by speaking out it is likely that he would have difficulty convincing the police of his innocence. It could easily be argued that a priest who was willing to violate the secrets of the confessional to protect himself might well be a liar, too.

The film undoubtedly benefits from the superbly atmospheric black-

and-white photography of Robert Burks and extensive use of Quebec locations and interiors, ranging from famous landmarks to some of the city's quaintly narrow, winding streets. However, this serves to point up the artificiality of the film's dependence on English-speaking, American stars. There is hardly a line of French spoken in the entire film, while Anne Baxter is badly miscast, in an impossible role, as the priest's former girlfriend who still loves him. Montgomery Clift gives a solid and convincing performance, though Hitchcock found him extremely difficult to work with, and his character lacks the kind of interior and spiritual qualities that could have lifted the film above the banality and contrivance of the plot.

Most interesting of all is O.E. Hasse's compelling performance as the immigrant sacristan murderer. Initially frightened and horrified at what he had done, we first see him in the church, then delivering his anguished confession to his friend, the priest. (The murder was not planned and happened when he was caught attempting a robbery.) But we witness a gradual change in his character as the film develops. When he observes his friend becoming progressively more implicated in the crime and no mention is made of the confession, he sees an opportunity to protect himself by planting additional evidence to implicate the priest further. He becomes more crafty and evil and even shoots his own wife in a last desperate attempt to protect his guilty secret. He is finally caught and dies, appropriately enough, in the arms of his friend, the priest. He certainly deserves to be included in any list of memorable Hitchcock villains.

Between the time that Hitch had finished *I Confess* (in 1952) and the beginning of shooting on his next picture, *Dial M for Murder*, in the summer of 1953, a lot of changes had taken place in Hollywood. This was the beginning of a period of technical innovation and experimentation that would continue throughout the rest of the 1950s. A number of new techniques, including Cinerama and 3-D, had just been introduced that would prove to be successful, at least temporarily, in halting the postwar fall in movie audiences. 20th Century-Fox was just completing its first CinemaScope features in the summer of 1953 and arch-rival Paramount would have its first VistaVision production, *White Christmas*, ready for release the following year.

In addition, there was a widespread increase in the number of features filmed in colour – the percentage of colour had doubled from 21 per cent in 1950–1 to 43 per cent in 1953, and the introduction of a new Eastman Color negative meant that it was no longer necessary to film with the special, three-strip Technicolor cameras (as Hitchcock had done on both *Rope* and *Under Capricorn*). Many leading directors were working in colour for the first time, and often their first colour feature was also filmed in one of the new processes.

Since Warner Bros had had a big hit with its 3-D version of *House of Wax* in the spring of 1953, the studio bosses then pressured Hitchcock into filming *Dial M for Murder* in 3-D, though by the time the picture was ready for release, early in 1954, the 3-D fad had passed and it was screened mainly in a standard version. (By then it was also clear that CinemaScope was the more viable process and Warners shifted its position accordingly; thus both George Cukor, with *A Star is Born*, and Elia Kazan, with *East of Eden*, found themselves shooting their first colour features in CinemaScope at Warners in 1954, and it is quite likely that, had Hitchcock remained at this studio, he too would have been forced to shoot his next picture in 'Scope.) It is possible that such considerations played a part in Hitch's decision to leave Warner Bros and sign a lucrative new contract with Paramount in the summer of 1953.

According to actress Grace Kelly, during the filming of *Dial M for Murder* Hitchcock was already preparing his next picture. This would be his first for Paramount, *Rear Window*, and Kelly would again be the co-star. Hitchcock alone was quick to recognize the great potential of the young actress, which had hardly been tapped in her previous pictures, and was even unappreciated at MGM, who had her under contract, but kept loaning her out. His relationship with Kelly, even more than that with Joan Fontaine previously, demonstrated how sensitive, considerate and helpful he could be in his handling of relatively inexperienced actors. She had not been happy with her experience with previous directors Fred Zinnemann (on *High Noon*) and the veteran John Ford (on *Mogambo*). As she later recalled, 'Working with Hitchcock was a tremendous experience . . . As an actor I learned a tremendous amount about motion picture making. He gave me a great deal of confidence in myself.'

In filming *Dial M for Murder*, Hitch had quickly realized that the special qualities of the original play and its dramatic effectiveness would be ruined by any attempt to 'open it out' as is often done in film adaptations. He decided, instead, to remain faithful to the original and shoot virtually the entire film on a single large apartment set similar to that in the play. This also made it easier to control any problems that might develop in the 3-D filming. Benefiting from his outstanding technical expertise and past experience in coping with difficult technical challenges – such as the long takes in *Rope*, filmed at the same Warners studio – the shooting was completed fairly quickly and smoothly. Of course, he did avoid the usual gimmicks associated with 3-D films, such

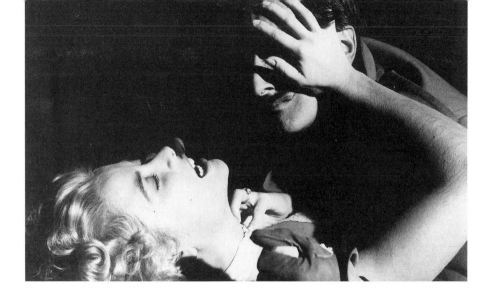

In the most violent sequence of *Dial M for Murder* (1954) the hired killer, Anthony Dawson, attacks Grace Kelly and attempts to strangle her with a scarf. In desperation she reaches back across the desk and grasps a pair of scissors which she then plunges into his back. This was a difficult scene to shoot in 3-D, and Hitchcock hated the process, but enjoyed working with Grace Kelly for the first time.

as objects suddenly thrown or thrust at the movie audience. But there was one notable 3-D sequence, the most dramatic in the film, when the heroine is attacked and almost strangled, but manages to kill her assailant by stabbing him in the back with a pair of scissors. Apparently, Hitchcock took an entire week to rehearse and film this short scene, but the results more than justified this.

Although the completed picture hardly qualifies as one of Hitch's best, it is effective and gripping from beginning to end, with few slack moments, and is more concentrated and considerably shorter (at only 88 minutes) than the original play. (It is Hitchcock's shortest American picture, aside from *Rope*.) Though lacking in originality, the film clearly demonstrates Hitchcock's qualities as a craftsman-director and was much appreciated, for example, by fellow director François Truffaut who was impressed by 'the cutting, the rhythm and the direction of the players'. In fact, it turned out to be the most successful of all his Warner Bros pictures at the box office, but by the time it opened, in the spring of 1954, Hitch had already completed his first Paramount film, *Rear Window*, and was well on his way to reviving his career. This was a major step towards what were to be the most successful and productive years of his life.

6

1953-55: Paramount

From *Rear Window* to *The Man Who Knew Too Much*

When Hitchcock arrived at Paramount in the autumn of 1953, he appeared especially confident and optimistic regarding his current and future film plans. Although he had been given a fair degree of freedom, his years at Warner Bros had not been successful on the whole, and he had never felt truly at home there. His seven year association with the studio had begun in the late 1940s when Warners agreed to distribute Transatlantic's productions in the US (*Rope* was even filmed at the Warner studio). However, he had occasionally been forced to use actresses such as Ruth Roman (in *Strangers on a Train*) and Anne Baxter (in *I Confess*), and had not been happy with another Warners star, Jane Wyman, in *Stage Fright*. And he had especially resented having to shoot *Dial M for Murder* in 3-D.

Perhaps his lack of success had been complicated by a sort of 'mid-life crisis' during these years. However, it soon became apparent that he was back in peak form during the filming of *Rear Window*, his first Paramount picture, with two of his favourite stars, Grace Kelly and James Stewart. As Stewart later recalled, 'The whole production of *Rear Window* went so very smoothly. The set and every part of the film were so well designed, and he felt so comfortable with everyone associated with it, that we all felt confident about its success.'

Hitchcock had brought with him cameraman Robert Burks and his camera operator, Leonard South, from Warner Bros and would soon succeed in assembling his own, favourite production team, most of whom would remain with him for the next ten years or so. These included leading Paramount costume designer Edith Head (who had previously worked with him on *Notorious*), editor George Tomasini and assistant director Herbert Coleman, who soon graduated to second unit director and then associate producer. (Composer Bernard Herrmann would join him on his third Paramount movie, *The Trouble with Harry*, late in 1954.)

In addition, Hitchcock collaborated closely with writer John Michael Hayes who would also script his next three films. Hayes' contribution was especially important here. As with *Strangers on a Train*, Hitch could clearly see the cinematic possibilities contained in Cornell Woolrich's original story. But whereas on the earlier film, a rambling and diffuse novel had to be tightened up and concentrated to maintain an effectively *noir*ish atmosphere on the screen (in black-and-white, of course), here the goal was virtually the opposite: a relatively succinct short story was opened up, expanded, even brightened up a bit, and filmed in colour, thus taking it out of the realm of *film noir*. Hitchcock's idea of making use of a more ordinary-looking, everyday setting as the scene of the murder fitted in with his own offbeat sense of humour and of the irony of the situation. And perhaps the most important new ingredient in Hitchcock's approach was the addition of an entirely new character, of the incapacitated hero's girlfriend, not found in the original story. Thus, one can see a neat link here between Hitchcock's ideas as to how he intended to adapt the story to the screen and his desire to find a role for Grace Kelly in his next film. In fact, her character is crucial to the new, lighter tone of the picture, which has been effectively transformed into a comedy thriller while still retaining many of the original story's darker moments.

Writer Hayes recalls that Hitchcock had recognized early on how important it was for him to meet Kelly and spend some time with her in order to gain a better understanding of what she might be capable of as an actress and of those special qualities that had never before been captured on the screen in her few previous roles: a sophistication and elegance and perhaps slightly cool looking exterior, while suggesting at the same time a vitality and sensuality hidden beneath the surface.

It was, of course, the first time that a film role was specially written for her, so it is not surprising that she fitted it so well. She would play a society girl and top New York model. As a former model herself, Kelly comes across as incredibly elegant and glamorous, yet witty and intelligent and even courageous too. (One of the most suspenseful moments in the film comes when she slips into the suspected murderer's apartment in search of a vital piece of evidence and we, like Stewart, are forced to watch helplessly as the murderer returns unexpectedly and catches her.)

In addition, as with *Dial M for Murder*, her costumes once again provided Hitchcock with his best opportunity to introduce a note of colour into the film, with the help of Edith Head, of course, and provides another example of his meticulous attention to detail. As he described his 'colour experiment' on *Dial M* to Truffaut, 'I dressed her in very gay and bright colours at the beginning of the picture, and as the plot thickened her clothes became gradually more sombre.' Similarly, on *Rear Window*, 'every costume was indicated when he sent me the finished script.' Edith Head later recalled. 'There was a reason for every colour, every style, and he was absolutely certain about everything he settled on. For one scene he saw her in pale green, for another in white chiffon, for another in gold.'

However, it was James Stewart, Hitchcock's favourite American actor, in the second of his four films for the director, who was the real star of the picture. He is hardly ever off the screen and gives a real virtuoso performance as the tall, convalescing, freelance photographer, awkwardly confined by a broken leg to a wheelchair, who suspects that a murder has been committed by one of his neighbours living across the courtyard from his Greenwich Village apartment.

Also crucial to the success of the film of course, was the interaction between the two leads. Fortunately, they got on extremely well. There is a lively give-and-take between the irritable photographer, suffering from the summer heat (and sheer boredom), and Kelly as his attractive, but strong-willed, fiancée who appears at regular intervals to keep him company and becomes involved in his amateur sleuthing. (The sophisticated banter between them worked so well that Hitch partly recycled the relationship in two of the best of his later films, *Vertigo* and *North by Northwest*.)

Finally, Thelma Ritter was superbly cast in the main supporting role as the down-to-earth and cynical nurse. Not only does she give her usual excellent performance but she also contributes a bit of authentic flavour, too, providing the film with its only New York accent.

Although *Rear Window* represented a new start for Hitchcock at Paramount, the film also marked the end of his special use of studio settings as part of a long tradition which can be traced back to the beginnings of his career in the 1920s. It especially stands out as the last and best of that group of American films mainly confined to a single studio set, from *Lifeboat* to *Rope* and *Dial M for Murder*.

In spite of the apparently realistic look of the setting, it would have been virtually impossible to shoot this picture on location. By filming in the studio, Hitchcock gained the total control over the setting which he required, which involved both day and night sequences and creating the illusion that the events in the film take place during a particularly hot and humid summer heat wave. Ironically, *Rear Window* would be the only picture that he filmed during the winter months throughout the 1950s, reflecting the fact that he was now shooting more on location and

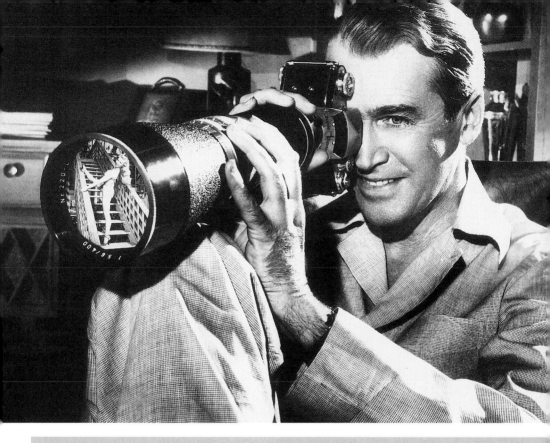

James Stewart spies on his neighbours while confined to his wheelchair – this still captures the voyeuristic theme which is central to *Rear Window* (1954). Here Hitchcock also exploits the comedy of a sexual reversal of roles: the extremely tall Stewart appears awkward, helpless and dependent on the regular visits of his quite practical, efficient and independent-minded girl friend played by the beautiful, young Grace Kelly in a role tailor-made for her.

preferred to film outdoors during the warmer months of the year. (His last previous winter filming had occurred on two of his most studio-bound pictures of the 1940s, *The Paradine Case* and *Rope*.)

Hitch was eager to start filming at Paramount after signing his new contract with the studio in 1953, but was still involved in shooting his last Warners production, *Dial M for Murder*. Thus he realized that he would first be free during the winter months and was attracted to the idea of finding a suitable studio subject. Grace Kelly recalled him enthusiastically talking about the new project he was developing, with special reference to the 'fabulous set' he had envisaged, even before he told her about the part he was planning for her.

'We had to build a set containing thirty-one other apartments (which) Stewart sees from his (*rear*) *window*,' Hitchcock explained to an interviewer. 'An ostensibly one-room set (representing Stewart's own studio flat) turned out to be almost the biggest one ever made at Paramount. We had twelve of these apartments completely furnished. We could never have gotten them properly lit in a real location.' The set design was credited to art director Joseph McMillan Johnson, assisted by Sam Comer and Ray Mayer.

Rear Window, therefore, appealed to him as a subject specially designed for studio filming, yet suitably original in conception and providing meaty roles for his two favorite American stars – the kind of project which only he could do. If it came off, it should prove a good start to his relationship with the new studio. In fact, with the script knocked into shape by John Michael Hayes and the set completed, he was able to start filming *Rear Window* without delay, less than two months after *Dial M* had wrapped.

Art director Joseph McMillan Johnson who had previously collaborated with Hitchcock on *The Paradine Case*, here designed an impressive 'composite set' for *Rear Window* to accommodate Hitchcock's needs.

Representing the entire back courtyard and apartments looking out on it, this was one of the largest sets ever built on the Paramount back lot. As conceived by him, the camera was confined to James Stewart's apartment throughout virtually the entire film. On the one hand, we observe the objective reality of his life in the apartment during the period of a few days during a summer heatwave, and on the other there is the more subjective reality of his fragmented glimpses of the lives of his neighbours observed across the courtyard with the help of binoculars and a powerful telephoto lens (a useful piece of his photographer's equipment). Frequently they are seen, but not heard, accompanied by his own interpretation of what he sees; often his comments are lighthearted or flippant, but become deadly serious when he begins to suspect that a murder may have been committed. (A minor weakness in the film is the fact that his neighbours tend to be presented in a rather too clichéd and facile manner, a bit too obviously representing a typical cross-section of big city life, and a very Hollywoody view of Greenwich Village.)

Hitchcock himself has drawn attention to the subtle way in which the pacing of the film has been carefully worked out: the 'rhythm of the cutting', in particular, speeds up as the plot thickens.

> At the beginning, life is going on quite normally. The tempo is leisurely. There's a bit of conflict between the man and the girl. And then gradually the first suspicion grows and it increases. And naturally as you reach the last third of your picture the events have to pile on top of each other . . .

Especially brilliant is his handling of the climax when Stewart is attacked by the murderer and attempts to defend himself by firing off flashbulbs to temporarily blind the man and is then caught after he is thrown from the window and lands hard on the pavement breaking his other leg.

Of interest, too, is the fact that *Rear Window* marks the end of Hitchcock's filming in the old screen format. Here he demonstrated the effectiveness of shooting in the 3×4 ratio, which seems just right, given the shape of the window(s) framing much of the action and the carefully constructed set with its strong vertical and horizontal lines. His next three films would be shot in colour and in Paramount's new VistaVision widescreen process, making use of locations in France, England, North Africa and New England. Though he would return to the old format and black-and-white for *The Wrong Man* and *Psycho*, they too would be largely filmed on location (with studio interiors only). Never again would Hitchcock experiment with studio shooting of an entire film.

On *Rear Window* one can sense the emergence of a more confident and mature Hitchcock, functioning effectively as a producer-director and controlling every aspect of the film. This is the kind of personal project

that one could not imagine being made by any other director in Hollywood. Filmed on a $2 million budget, it turned out to be a smash hit and
his biggest success since *Notorious*, not only at the box office, but also
with the critics and the Academy. It was Oscar-nominated for sound
recording, cinematography (Burks), script (Hayes) and director.

Such was the pace of his filming at this time, however, that by the
time *Rear Window* was released he was already in the middle of shooting his next film with Grace Kelly, *To Catch a Thief*. She too was at the
peak of her short movie career. During 1953–4 she would make seven
films in rapid succession, including the three with Hitchcock. She
received the New York Film Critics award for her performances in three
pictures released in 1954 – *Dial M for Murder*, *The Country Girl* and

Two of Hitch's favourite stars, Grace Kelly and Cary Grant, appeared
together in *To Catch a Thief*. Though Grant was almost twice her age, they
made a handsome couple. Director and stars apparently enjoyed filming on
the Riviera in the summer of 1954. Aside from a few scenes for *Topaz* (1969),
this was the only Hitchcock picture filmed in France. Grant was persuaded to
emerge from a relatively brief (two-year) retirement to play the role of
retired cat burglar John Robie, but was then available for one last, memorable Hitchcock role in *North by Northwest* a few years later.

Rear Window. (Her Oscar was awarded for *The Country Girl.*) In addition, the tremendous success of *Rear Window* was reflected in the box office rating of its two stars. James Stewart rose from number four on the list of top box office stars in 1954 to number one in 1955 (when Paramount's *Strategic Air Command* was also a big hit), while Grace Kelly appeared on the list for the only time in the number two spot, having also starred in the highly successful *The Country Girl* along with her third Hitchcock hit, *To Catch a Thief.*

For Hitchcock too, this was his most prolific period as a Hollywood film-maker. Having directed only two features during 1950–2, he suddenly demonstrated a new enthusiasm, shooting his next four features – three of them starring Miss Kelly – within the space of a year and a half from mid-1953 to the end of 1954.

Having initially made himself at home on the Paramount back lot on *Rear Window*, his second production for the studio represented a very different kind of experiment. *To Catch a Thief* was one of the first pictures to be filmed with the newly-developed VistaVision cameras.

Towards the end of 1953, at around the same time that Hitchcock was filming *Rear Window*, 20th Century-Fox had had a big success with its first CinemaScope releases. Paramount responded by developing its own rival widescreen process, VistaVision, and the new cameras were ready for use by the time of Hitchcock's next production. In fact, the new subject had actually been suggested to him by Paramount – the picturesque Riviera settings would obviously be ideal for demonstrating the special qualities of the new process, which involved exposing a larger negative image – eight sprocket holes wide – to get a much sharper image on the screen. (The VistaVision camera used standard 35mm film, but it ran through the camera sideways, rather than vertically.)

In view of Hitch's preference for varying his projects from film to film, it is not surprising that he was persuaded by Paramount to follow *Dial M* and *Rear Window* with a somewhat lighter, entertaining comedy-thriller. He would have appreciated the obvious commercial appeal of *To Catch a Thief*, with the opportunity to pair two of his favourite stars and shoot in the south of France.

With the decline in the old studio system, there was a clear move towards filming increasingly in colour (and widescreen) and on location, as well as abroad, where costs were often lower. Thus, Hitchcock's own attraction to location filming clearly fitted in with this trend. *To Catch a Thief*, for example, was one of the first widescreen pictures to be filmed abroad, and this was naturally considered to be an important selling point by Paramount. Thus, the posters for the film stated, 'You'll feel that you're actually on the beautiful Riviera in Vistavision.'

The picture presented yet another variation on the theme of the wrongly accused man who sets out to clear himself. Cary Grant plays a highly successful, but retired, cat burglar who realizes that he is suspected by the police because a new thief is imitating his methods, and that he is the only person who can prove his innocence by catching the imposter himself. Appropriately enough, Cary Grant was persuaded to come out of a two-year retirement from the screen to play the leading role opposite Grace Kelly. (Having succeeded in getting Grant to resume his movie career, Hitchcock would benefit four years later, too, when the actor starred in *North by Northwest*, the last and best of his four films with him.)

Grant clearly had fun with the lead role in the Arsène Lupin or Raffles tradition of the gentleman thief, and he and Kelly made an attractive couple on screen. A stylish, entertaining and charming film, it provided opportunities for a number of Hitchcock's most dependable collaborators. John Michael Hayes again supplied the appropriately witty dialogue, full of sexual hints and *double entendres*, for the slightly offbeat romance between the rich young American heiress and the sophisticated thief to whom she is attracted, in spite of the fact that he is almost old enough to be her father. Robert Burks made the most of the film's photographic opportunities and won the Oscar for colour cinematography, while art director Joseph McMillan Johnson and costume designer Edith Head were also nominated for their contributions to the film's impeccably colourful and glossy appearance. Miss Head, in fact, recalls the picture as one of her own special favourites. She provided Kelly with an appropriate selection of stunning gowns and summery outfits and had special fun with an elaborate costume ball that takes place on the climactic final evening: Kelly was fitted out in a hoop-skirted, gold lamé ballgown and period wig.

Hitchcock was already well advanced on his next project, an adaptation of the novel *The Trouble with Harry*, by Jack Trevor Story, before he had completed shooting on *To Catch a Thief* in August 1954. Not only had Hayes completed much of the script by this time, but Hitchcock was already making plans to begin his filming on location in Vermont: since he wished to capture the multi-coloured foliage of a New England Indian summer on film, he knew that the VistaVision cameras had to be ready to roll by the end of September.

Rear Window had just been released and looked like being a big success. Thus, he felt more confident about his decision to take a break from the big star movies he had been making and indulge himself with a small scale, more intimate picture and story based on that very British type of black humour that particularly appealed to him and would be a staple element of his television series during the coming years. It would be his first comedy since he first took a stab at an American screwball style of filming with *Mr and Mrs Smith* fourteen years earlier. By shooting the new picture relatively quickly and cheaply, on a modest budget of about $1 million, with no major stars in the cast, but in colour and VistaVision, he expected that it would be appealing enough to American audiences at least to break even.

The farcical plot revolves around the sudden, unexplained appearance of a dead body in a wooded glade on a typical, bright sunny day in early autumn. The leaves are just changing colour and the picturesque rural setting provides an incongruously colourful backdrop to the film's macabre themes of death, and possible murder, and how best to dispose of an unwanted corpse. The general tone is established by the opening dialogue between the elderly Miss Gravely (Mildred Natwick) and her neighbour, a retired sea captain, played by Edmund Gwenn:

> *Shot No.42.* Medium shot of the captain holding the feet of the corpse, which he is dragging to the nearby wood.
>
> *Miss Gravely* enters the shot and looks down: 'What seems to be the trouble, Captain?'
>
> He lets go of one foot: 'Well it's what you might call an unavoidable accident. He's dead.'
>
> *Insert.* Miss Gravely's foot prodding arm of dead man: 'I would say that he was. Of course, that's an-unprofessional opinion.'

During the course of the film it emerges that the eponymous Harry has been hit over the head with a milk bottle, shot at and clobbered with the heel of a woman's shoe, and a number of the local residents each think that they may have been responsible for his death. Thus, his corpse is repeatedly buried and dug up, hidden in a wood and in a bath tub, dragged about and tripped over and even models for the local artist. He is undressed and cleaned up and finally put back where he was first discovered in time for the final fade-out.

Unfortunately, excessive rain during the month of October meant that Hitch was unable to accomplish all the location filming that he had originally planned. He was forced to depend more on studio sequences and this contributed to the film's already rather static quality. He was disappointed by the movie's failure at the box office, attributing this to the lack of major stars, but the characters never really come alive on the screen, in spite of the efforts of the cast, including most notably Edmund Gwenn in one of his last movie roles and a young Shirley MacLaine in her very first. It also benefited from a lively score from composer Bernard Herrmann, here working with Hitchcock for the first time.

The public's response to the film was not helped by the fact that Paramount really did not know how to promote it, emphasizing the fact that it was very different from the usual Hitchcock thriller, 'The *Unexpected* from Hitchcock', while drawing attention to the colourful and attractive look of the picture – 'What Hitchcock did for the Riviera in *To Catch a Thief*, he does now for New England in VistaVision'.

However, *The Trouble with Harry* was the only flop out of the six pictures he made for Paramount in the 1950s, for he immediately bounced back with another hit, returning to the more familiar mainstream filming with *The Man Who Knew Too Much* starring James Stewart and Doris Day. This time he took the VistaVision cameras to Morocco and London to shoot a loose remake of his own 1934 picture. This is one of Hitchcock's relatively few American pictures dealing with the family, and he obviously could not resist the temptation to poke fun at the behaviour of a typically All-American, middle-class family from the Midwest on their first holiday abroad in exotic North Africa. It also provided a good excuse for including some stunning location photography. Critic Jean-Luc Godard, for one, was greatly impressed. As he wrote in *Cahiers du Cinéma* in 1956:

> When he leaves the studio to shoot on location, the director of *To Catch a Thief* allows his actors more freedom, lets his camera linger on a landscape, seizes neatly and firmly on every droll character or bizarre object to come his way. The scenes in the bedroom, the Arab café, the two police offices (French and English), the taxidermist's shop, the Presbyterian chapel, the concert or the embassy ought, if they are logical, to make all the Buñuels and Zavattinis of this world pale with envy.

Only a few years on from *Rear Window*, Stewart now looks a bit older as a family man, father and doctor, who changes during the course of the film from the relatively easy-going American tourist of the opening reels to the tougher and more determined figure of the second half coping with police and detectives and tracking foreign agents as he sets out to rescue his kidnapped son. Doris Day is also convincing in one of her rare dramatic roles of the 1950s as the mother and wife placed under a great strain. And she gets to sing, too: the sentimental song 'Che Sera Sera', specially composed for the film (and winner of the Best Song Oscar for 1956) is worked into the plot as a means of contact between mother and son in the picture's final climax. In fact, there are two dramatic climaxes. Best known of all is the attempted assassination filmed at the Albert Hall, which demonstrates Hitchcock's flawless sense of pacing and ability to build up the tension through music and editing with virtually no dialogue. (For this famous Hitchcock set-piece sequence, composer

Small town doctor James Stewart, on holiday in Morocco, finds himself plunged into the midst of an international conspiracy and assassination plot when he goes to the aid of an Arab who has been stabbed in the back in Hitchcock's 1956 remake of *The Man Who Knew Too Much*. Frenchman Daniel Gélin whispers his dying words into Stewart's ear as a friendly English couple, Bernard Miles and Brenda de Banzie (partially hidden), look on.

Bernard Herrmann makes a rare appearance in front of the cameras as the conductor of the orchestra.) The film concludes with a real tearjerker ending as the son is rescued through the combined efforts of his parents, and the family are happily reunited.

Less than vintage Hitchcock, this film appears, in retrospect, as an appropriate way for him to have brought to a close the most commercial phase in his American career. He had shot five films in a row in colour, one in 3-D and three in VistaVision. Three were big hits, with one smaller success (*Dial M for Murder*) and only one flop, while four were scripted by the same writer (Hayes). Though the films were popular with audiences, they were not among Hitchcock's best efforts, with the sole exception of *Rear Window*, his only notable production since *Strangers on a Train*. He appeared to be in danger of lapsing permanently into a commercial rut, turning out colourful and popular pictures with leading stars that fitted easily into the Hollywood mould.

Thus, far from serving as a demonstration of the best qualities of the mature Hitchcock, *The Man Who Knew Too Much* is really symptomatic of that particularly disappointing phase of his career. And the all too obvious weaknesses of the film are made even more apparent by comparing it with his own, earlier version of the same story. (It is certainly possible to imagine Hitchcock shooting a much tougher, imaginative, less commercial version without expensive stars and in black-and-white, even in the 1950s.) He himself may have been well aware of this danger, since the year 1955 marks the end of this phase in his development.

Surprisingly, many critics readily accept the fact that Hitchcock himself preferred the later version, due to a well known quote from the Truffaut book: 'Let's say that the first version was the work of a talented amateur and the second was made by a professional.' (Spoto even uses this quote to open his chapter on the film in his book *The Art of Alfred Hitchcock*.) However, Hitchcock gave many interviews throughout his long career and often said different things to different interviewers. Thus, David Castell quotes him in 1972, suggesting that he specially liked the earlier version: 'I think it was more spontaneous – it had less logic. Logic is dull: you always lose the bizarre and spontaneous.'

Ray Durgnat (unintentionally?) echoes Hitchcock's own words when he favours the first as '. . . faster, more irrational, and sports a poetic flair for the bizarre, while the latter is more elaborate, not to say plodding . . .' On the other hand, Robin Wood, a more 'literary' critic, agrees with Spoto and asserts that it is incomprehensible to him that anyone could take the opposite view 'outside the most flagrant chauvinism' i.e., preferring earlier, British Hitchcock to the later American films. He thus misses the whole point – that the later version is one of Hitchcock's weakest fifties films. He enjoys analysing the treatment of the characters at length, apparently blind to the fact that it is just this attempt to make them into more fully rounded and psychologically convincing portraits, especially the mother, as played by Doris Day, that is the source of the trouble. As John Russell Taylor succinctly notes, the film has become 'weighed down with the sort of psychological elaboration which it cannot really bear.' The first version occupies a very special place in the Hitchcock *oeuvre* reflecting a new confidence in his abilities as he begins to find his own voice as a film-maker in the mid-1930s, a first step towards his remarkable series of thrillers during 1935–8. The later film, however, though accomplished technically and reasonably entertaining, is obviously aimed at a large international audience. All the rough edges from the original have been smoothed out, and the result is far from Hitch at his best.

1955 was also the year when Hitchcock launched his highly popular television series, 'Alfred Hitchcock Presents', and although this is not the place for a proper discussion of the series, it should be noted that he directed twenty segments himself, averaging about three per year during the 1955–60 period, while personally introducing all the programmes. Apparently, he was inspired to adopt a similar tone and dry sense of humour as that seen in the offbeat comedy shorts of Robert Benchley, such as 'How to Sleep' and 'The Sex Life of the Polyp'. As a natural extension of his well known cameo appearances, these made him more of a national celebrity than ever before.

The series provided him with the opportunity to direct teleplays adapted from stories by some of his favourite mystery writers and to make additional use of actors from his feature films, such as Joseph Cotten, Vera Miles, Claude Rains and John Williams. His involvement with the series also served to orient him more towards specifically American themes and stars than ever before. His television activity may have actually helped him in selecting subjects for his features and gave him a new impetus to accomplish on film what he could not do on TV. In 1955, sixteen years after his arrival in the US, he finally adopted American citizenship at the same time that he appeared to have gained greater confidence in dealing with American subjects. During 1956–64, for example, not one of his films took place outside the US, in marked contrast to the international flavour of the 1952–5 years. Not only is his choice of subjects impeccable, but also he suddenly appears to have recaptured that creative drive that had temporarily deserted him as he embarked on what was arguably the most remarkable period of film-making of his entire career.

7

1956-64:
The Peak Years in America

From *The Wrong Man* to *Marnie*

Hitchcock became an American citizen in April 1955, *To Catch a Thief* was released in August, and his new television series premiered in October. With *The Man Who Knew Too Much* completed by the end of the year and likely to be another hit, Hitchcock was already deeply involved in his next project with writers Maxwell Anderson and Angus MacPhail back at Warners. According to biographer John Russell Taylor, Hitchcock apparently felt that he owed Warner Bros another film. ('He had completed the work required of him under his contract . . . but was not satisfied that he had given them full value for money.') Here he had made his last two black-and-white pictures in the early 1950s, so it is not too surprising that he should choose to return to the same studio to make a serious dramatic film in black-and-white at this time. There were obvious thematic links with *Strangers on a Train* and especially, *I Confess*, about a wrongly accused man, as well as with earlier films such as *Spellbound* and his first important feature *The Lodger* in 1926.

In retrospect, one can recognize that this new film, *The Wrong Man*, marked a major turning point for him. This was not just a special, one-off project, but rather the first of a memorable series of pictures. During these years he managed to come up with one original film idea after

Intense concentration shows on the faces of Alfred Hitchcock and his star, Henry Fonda, as they prepare to shoot a scene for *The Wrong Man*, on location in New York in 1956. The film was closely based on the true story of a man falsely accused and arrested for a crime he did not commit. As Hitch later explained, 'I thought the story would make an interesting picture if all the events were shown from the viewpoint of the innocent man, describing his suffering as a result of a crime committed by someone else . . .'

another, remarkable in their quality and diversity and reflecting his own preference for varying his projects from film to film. Yet they were generally characterized by a darker, more serious tone recalling the best of his earlier American films such as *Shadow of a Doubt*, *Notorious* and *Strangers on a Train*. (Of the six pictures filmed by Hitchcock during 1956–64, only one, *North by Northwest*, resembled the kind of colourful and entertaining thrillers of the 1953–5 years, and even that film, too, would emerge as a special example of this popular genre.)

One can only speculate on the reasons for the transformation. Although Hitchcock's creative powers were still formidable, he had reached an age (his late fifties) when he must have begun to realize that he did not have all that many years left to revitalize his career and achieve a quality of film-making to match his recent commercial success.

Hitchcock's six features during 1956–64 were made for four different Hollywood studios. Two were shot in black-and-white, two in Vista-Vision and two in widescreen colour. They were derived from a variety of sources, both fictional and real life, and ranged from adaptations of novels to a freely-adapted short story ('The Birds') and included two film originals. Hitchcock retained the leading members of his production team on five of the films, though there were different scriptwriters on each: he was generally fortunate in matching the appropriate writers to each project, after a couple of false starts. (It is perhaps significant that he made a break with John Michael Hayes, who had scripted four films in a row for him and was very much identified with that mid-50s, popular phase in his development.)

All were shot extensively on location in the US, making use of a wide variety of settings and divided equally between the East and West Coast (three films each). They ranged from quick and inexpensive black-and-white filming (*The Wrong Man*, *Psycho*) to relatively lavish colour and VistaVision with a large and expensive cast, including a number of top stars (*North by Northwest*). The casts included some established stars (Fonda, Stewart, Grant) as well as newer, younger players, and relatively few 'repeaters' (only Vera Miles and Tippi Hedren in two films each).

In fact, there was a special significance in Hitchcock's decision to return to black-and-white filming at Warners at this particular time. During the 1950s and well into the 1960s colour was still disliked by many of the leading directors and cameramen (though Hitchcock was not one of this group), and black-and-white was still identified closely with serious dramatic subjects on the screen. The pressures on *all* Hollywood directors to shoot *all* their films in colour, as well as in one of the new widescreen processes, during 1954–5 in particular, had begun to ease by 1956 as the studio executives realized that the new technology alone was not sufficient to restore movie attendance to earlier levels and sustain it over the long term, and that there were some subjects that lent themselves to an intimate or black-and-white format which was less costly.

Thus, 20th Century-Fox, which had originally launched CinemaScope as an exclusively colour process, released its first black-and-white feature in CinemaScope (*Teenage Rebel*) in 1956, for example, and a number of top directors who had worked in colour in 1954–5 returned to black-and-white around this time, including Billy Wilder (with *Love in the Afternoon* followed by *Witness for the Prosecution* and *Some Like It Hot*), Robert Wise with *Somebody Up There Likes Me* and Anthony Mann with *Men in War* followed by *The Tin Star*. Joining Hitchcock at Warners in 1956, where they too reverted to black-and-white, were Elia Kazan with *Baby Doll* followed by *A Face in the Crowd* and Mervyn LeRoy with *The Bad Seed*, based on the play by Maxwell Anderson, who had simultaneously been hired by Hitchcock to script *his* film *The Wrong Man*. By signing up the distinguished, veteran playwright, along with the actor Henry Fonda, who was generally identified with serious dramatic roles on the screen, Hitchcock made it quite clear that his new film, based on a true story, and shot in black-and-white, would represent a radical break from the kind of glossy and entertaining thrillers with which he had become identified during recent years.

Demonstrating that he was totally committed to the kind of low-key, naturalistic style the subject demanded, Hitchcock took his cast and crew to New York and shot much of the film on the very locations where the original events had taken place. (He even included, in minor roles, some of the people who had played a part in the real events a few years earlier.) In addition, he filmed, but decided not to use, his usual cameo appearance, having realized that it was not suitable, given the picture's sombre mood, and chose, instead, to introduce the film. He explains that although based on a true story, the events are stranger than any fiction.

The generally bleak tone is established in the opening reel as Fonda arrives home alone late at night from his job as bass player in a night club and finds his worried wife still awake, waiting up for him. There is a subtle hint here of her insecurity and vulnerability that will emerge more strongly in the second half of the film. But most compelling of all is the carefully observed series of events that take place during the course of a single day when Fonda is first apprehended by the police on his own doorstep as the prime suspect for a number of hold-ups that have taken place during the past year.

Treating him in a firm, but reassuring, manner, they refuse to let him contact his wife or get any legal advice while building up a substantial body of circumstantial evidence against him. Thus, they gradually succeed in undermining his self-confidence. He appears quite passive and hardly objects to the way in which he is treated, including a police interrogation, visits to the shops that were robbed for an identity check, appearing in a police line-up and even writing out a note demanding money to test his handwriting. Finally, he is fingerprinted and put into a cell for the night. The next morning he is arraigned in court and hand-cuffed to another prisoner as he is driven off in a prison van, apparently faced with a long pre-trial period in jail, for his bail has been set at a ridiculously high figure.

As François Truffaut noted when reviewing the film in 1957, Hitch-cock has shot the picture in such a way as to make it almost impossible to identify with the hero. 'We are limited to the role of witnesses. We are at Fonda's side throughout, in his cell, in his home, in the car, on the street . . . This time (Hitchcock) wants the public to experience a different kind of emotional shock . . .'

Fonda quite superbly conveys the feeling of a fairly ordinary, trusting and honest man caught in a nightmarish situation, while Vera Miles is convincing, too, as the insecure wife who suffers a mental breakdown from the strain on their relationship and somehow comes to blame herself for what has happened. (In his observation of a typical American family under stress, Hitchcock has provided one interesting link with his previous film, *The Man Who Knew Too Much*, though they are quite different in other respects.)

The film is perhaps a cautionary tale, too, about the dangers of being a very conventional and almost anonymous person in dress and behaviour. It's as if the hero's very blandness and lack of 'distinguishing characteristics' allows his accusers to misidentify him, to see someone who isn't there, beginning with the neurotic lady clerk in the insurance office who first thinks' she recognizes him. Once she starts the ball rolling, as it were, and two other women in the office sort of agree with her, the situation gradually develops and escalates in a manner that is both predictable and tragic in its consequences.

The final, dramatic climax of *Vertigo* (1958) when Judy (Kim Novak) will suddenly fall to her death as Scotty (James Stewart) looks on in horror. One of Hitchcock's most remarkable and accomplished productions, scriptwriter Samuel Taylor has noted that 'Hitch knew exactly what he wanted to do in this film . . . I gave him the characters and the dialogue he needed and developed the story. But it was from first frame to last his film. There was no moment that he wasn't there . . .'

10344-NPS-7

If nothing in the second half of the picture quite matches up to the remarkable quality of the opening reels – and there is even a slight shift in focus to concentrate on the deterioration in the wife's condition – yet the work as a whole is a remarkable and unexpected achievement for Hitchcock at this particular time. A generally under-rated picture, which some critics appear to have difficulty fitting into the Hitchcock *oeuvre*, it was not successful at the box office.

Hitchcock returned to Paramount (and colour) the following year (1957) for *Vertigo*, a very different kind of project from his previous Paramount productions. On the face of it, *Vertigo* was most closely related to his biggest 50s hit thus far, *Rear Window*, and the Paramount executives must have been pleased to learn that it would have some of the same story qualities as that picture, with the same star, James Stewart, as a *real* detective this time, and with plans for extensive location filming, in VistaVision, in and around San Francisco. In addition, his co-star would be the extremely attractive and popular young Kim Novak, on loanout from Columbia. (In 1956 she was the top-rated female star at the box office, aside from Marilyn Monroe, while Stewart was rated number three among the men behind William Holden and John Wayne.) Of course, they had no idea what Hitchcock was really up to – that he was planning to use the thriller format in a completely different and unusual way.

Perhaps Hitchcock also benefited from the fact that filming was delayed by his own illness at this time. A couple of other possible international productions had fallen through, thus leaving him free to mine that rich American vein in his Hollywood career, returning to northern California for the first time since *Shadow of a Doubt*. In addition, he had plenty of time to work on the script – loosely based on a French thriller, *D'Entre les Morts*, by Pierre Boileau and Thomas Narcejac who were best known in the US as the authors of *Les Diaboliques*.

Not surprisingly, Hitchcock initially experienced some problems with his writer collaborators. Maxwell Anderson had dropped out early on and Alec Coppel was only marginally more successful in giving Hitchcock what he wanted. Finally, playwright Samuel Taylor was hired. Though he had had little previous experience in films – most notably on Paramount's film version of his play *Sabrina Fair* in 1954 – he was a native of San Francisco and got on well with Hitchcock.

He recognized early on that his job was to work closely with Hitchcock and endeavour to give substance to the director's already precise ideas of what he visualized up on the screen – deepening the psychological treatment of the leading characters and strengthening the plot line to give the film greater narrative cohesion – rather than coming up with original ideas of his own. As Taylor later recalled, 'Working with him meant writing with him . . . Hitchcock never claimed to be a writer, but actually he did write his screenplays insofar as he visualized every scene in his mind and knew exactly how he wanted it to go . . .' But Taylor does claim that he introduced the new character of Stewart's sympathetic and long-suffering girlfriend (played by Barbara Bel Geddes). However, it is easy to spot the origin of her character in Stewart's similarly sophisticated and self-assured fiancée (played by Grace Kelly) in *Rear Window*.

In addition, since Hitchcock had strong ideas as to how he planned to make use of a number of specific settings, it was necessary for Taylor to accompany him: 'Hitchcock and I did a lot of location scouting together,' Taylor recalled. 'I spent two or three days at San Juan Bautista exploring the countryside and the mission and absorbing the spirit of the place. I sat down every day with Hitchcock and worked it out step-by-step.'

In addition to Taylor, *Vertigo* benefited from the fact that Hitchcock had assembled virtually his ideal team of collaborators for the film, including such regulars as Burks (camera), Tomasini (editor), Coleman (associate producer), Herrmann (score) and Head (costumes). But it also marked the return of Peggy Robertson, his favourite assistant, who would remain with him till the end of his career, and Henry Bumstead as the art director. (He had previously worked on *The Man Who Knew Too Much* and would later contribute to Hitch's last two American films – *Topaz* (1969) and *Family Plot* (1975).) Finally, there was Saul Bass. This was the first of a number of productions on which he would provide Hitchcock with some highly distinctive and original credit sequences, along with matching poster designs for publicizing the films, as well as occasional special contributions to the films themselves (most notably on *Psycho*). In each case Bass's titles serve to establish the general mood of the film before a word of dialogue has been spoken, effectively supported by Herrmann's dramatic opening music. For example, the theme of 'Vertigo' is expressed here through a series of multicoloured spiral shapes that first emerge from the eye of a woman's face seen in close-up.

The credits lead directly into the opening sequence without a break as a simple horizontal line across the screen becomes an iron bar and then is revealed as the top rung of a ladder leading onto a roof that is seized by a fugitive chased by the police. We are immediately plunged into the action. Stewart is the detective who misjudges his rooftop leap and is left clinging precariously to a gutter. As he looks down Hitchcock simulates his sudden fear and sense of vertigo through a combination of forward zoom downward and simultaneous reverse tracking, a special effect that he repeats later in the film.

In the scene that follows, the good-natured banter between Stewart and his attractive and intelligent girlfriend (Barbara Bel Geddes) immediately recalls *Rear Window*, and we discover that he was badly injured in the opening incident. He still walks with a slight limp and has left the police force, for he still suffers from acrophobia (a fear of heights). This combination of physical and psychological disability similarly links the two characters played by Stewart.

He is then hired by an old acquaintance who is worried about his wife Madeleine's apparent obsession with the past, her daily wanderings and possibly suicidal tendencies. Stewart is meant to follow discreetly and keep an eye on her, and it is arranged that he should see her for the first time at a swank local restaurant. She's stunningly beautiful, and Hitchcock gives an added punch to our (and Stewart's) first view of her: by creating a striking colour effect as her emerald green stole stands out against the deep burgundy coloured walls. Not only does Hitch make extensive use of a red-green opposition in the film's colour scheme, but also colours are used by him as an integral part of the 'double woman' pattern of the plot. (Following the death of Madeleine, in the second half of the film, Stewart will visit some of the same places, such as the restaurant, and when he discovers Judy, Madeleine's apparent 'double', he will dress her in the same clothes and same colours, which immediately carry us back to the earlier scenes.)

Costume designer Edith Head later recalled *Vertigo*, in particular, as a film on which Hitchcock had very specific ideas regarding the colours of the outfits to be worn by Kim Novak in the double role of Madeleine and Judy. These included 'the black and emerald green satin evening ensemble for the scene in the restaurant because it was an important story point. Both of the characters Kim played wore green; it was the colour of death. But other than colours, Hitchcock gives you a lot of room for your own ideas.'

Up to this point in the film there have been only a few brief exterior shots. Thus, there is a particular impact to the first brightly lit outdoor sequence as Stewart waits outside the plush apartment house for Madeleine to appear. It is as if Hitchcock is telling us the film really starts at this point. Again there is a special quality about our second clear glimpse of her in a florist's shop surrounded by multicoloured flowers, dressed in a sophisticated and chic grey suit. Bernard Herrmann's evocative score contributes to the strange, dream-like feel of this virtually dialogue-free sequence of scenes. Stewart continues to follow her to a chapel, then out to the adjoining garden and cemetery. Finally, she leads him to a local museum where the 'Portrait of Carlotta' provides a link with the previously observed headstone of Carlotta Valdes in the cemetery, then on to an old hotel where he thinks he sees her in the window, but she has mysteriously disappeared, and he is baffled.

Since this was Hitchcock's fourth picture filmed in VistaVision, he was well aware of the quality it could achieve on the screen. Clearly, *Vertigo* was a project that lent itself to a new creative approach, and it is apparent that he set out to make imaginative use of the VistaVision system in a manner that he had never attempted before.

There is a special 'feel' to '50s VistaVision productions, very different from that of the other 35mm widescreen systems at the time. Its significantly larger negative produced a sharper, less grainy image, and the excellent definition, combined with the use of wide angle lenses, meant that shots could be filled with lots of detail. Not surprisingly, Hitchcock was quick to appreciate this and went to great lengths to get all the little details in the film just right, from the flowers in the florist shop to the size, shape and colour of each individual car and truck passing along the street. And for the brief scene of the museum, he and the crew took special care to get the luminous effect he was after through a delicate combination of artificial lighting with the natural light shining through the glass ceiling.

Though the VistaVision colour photography gives a memorable quality to the many important location sequences in *Vertigo*, the system was also suited to special effects and soft focus effects. Thus, not only could Hitchcock vary the film's style, but he could also use the colours and special techniques at the same time to make important plot points. As he himself explained to François Truffaut,

> At the beginning of the picture, when James Stewart follows Madeleine to the cemetery, we gave her a dreamlike, mysterious quality by shooting through a fog filter. That gave us a green effect, like fog over the bright sunshine. Then, later on, when Stewart first meets Judy, I decided to make her live at the Empire Hotel in Post Street because it has a green neon sign flashing continually outside the window. So when the girl emerges from the bathroom, that green light gives her the same subtle, ghostlike quality. After focusing on Stewart, who's staring at her, we go back to the girl, but now we slip that soft effect away to indicate that Stewart's come back to reality . . .

The first day in which Stewart follows Madeleine sets the tone for the rest of the film, with its evocative background music and photography, including a careful placing of the camera and many long, smooth tracking shots. Hitchcock effectively creates a world of dreamlike fantasy on the screen, unlike any of his previous films. We identify closely with Stewart as he falls in love with this beautiful, mysterious girl. Later on they spend some time together after he rescues her from an apparent suicide attempt. But he is totally shattered when she does commit suicide, jumping from the bell tower at San Juan Bautista, for he had been unable to follow to stop her due to his acrophobia. (We later learn that 'Madeleine' is really a carefully groomed substitute as part of an elaborate plot to do away with the real wife.)

Stewart continues to be obsessed by Madeleine's memory even after he recovers from his mental breakdown (with the help of his sympathetic girlfriend). He keeps thinking that he sees her, in the restaurant or on the street, but turns out to be mistaken, as it is merely a woman wearing a similar suit or coat. Somehow he cannot believe that she is really dead – until one day he spots a girl in the street who really does look so like Madeleine that she could be her twin.

He follows her back to her hotel, introduces himself and manages to convince her of his genuine interest in seeing her again.

Having led Stewart from acrophobia through severe mental disorder, Hitchcock now carries his development of the character farther than he had dared in any of his previous films with the actor. Significantly, *Vertigo* is the last of their four films together, coming toward the end of Stewart's most flourishing years as a top star. In *Rope*, he was a lecturer given an opportunity to repudiate his own, dubious teachings after discovering the crime committed by two of his students, and in *Rear Window*, though he may be a bit of a voyeur, yet he does uncover a real murder. But in *Vertigo*, the hero's character is revealed as extremely nasty and unpleasant as the film develops. Hitchcock realizes that there is no way back. There can be no happy ending to this story.

Having discovered Judy and seen in her the possible fulfillment of his tragic lost love for Madeleine, he quickly drops any pretence as to his true feelings for Judy as Judy. His character becomes very strange and unsympathetic indeed. There is a nasty, obsessive quality to his behaviour as he controls Judy and forces her to agree to be transformed into 'Madeleine'. This means a change in hair style and colour (from reddish to platinum blonde) and an entirely new and more sophisticated wardrobe.

The transformation sequence itself, already referred to in the quote by Hitchcock above, takes place in her hotel room. The vulgarly attractive Judy has been changed into the cool and sophisticated beauty of Madeleine, most clearly symbolized by dressing her in the stylish grey suit worn by Madeleine when he had first fallen in love with her early in the film. (Amusingly enough, Edith Head recalls that Hitchcock had to be firm with Kim Novak who had actually objected to wearing the suit! 'For the scene in which she was to wear a grey suit and a white scarf with her platinum hair drawn back, Hitchcock had been very specific. He insisted that she was to look as if she just stepped out of the San Francisco fog – a woman of mystery and illusion.') When they kiss for the first time, the camera takes them dizzily round and around in a 360° pan using a back projection trick effect to take us back to the stable at San Juan Bautista just before Madeleine's suicide.

All of this has a heightened significance for the audience, for we, unlike the Stewart character, know that Judy and Madeleine are actually the same girl – revealed to us in a flashback.

There are obvious weaknesses in the film's plot, yet it is less a thriller than a powerful mixture of crime movie and black romantic fantasy, and one is carried along by the sheer power of Hitchcock's vision and the excellent performances of the cast. The more familiar one becomes with the film, and the more times one sees it, the less the obvious plot weaknesses seem to matter. Clearly, this is the ultimate Stewart-Hitchcock movie, occupying a very special place in the careers of both men. For example, during the postwar years and the 1950s in particular, Stewart very often played an extremely determined, even obsessive character, though often in a good cause – most clearly seen in his real life 'good guy' characters such as Glenn Miller (searching for that elusive, special big band sound) or young Lindbergh, dedicated to flying solo across the Atlantic, or the reporter in *Call Northside 777*, absolutely determined to prove that an innocent man has been wrongfully imprisoned. But in his Westerns, especially with Anthony Mann, the darker, more complex and troubled side of the Stewart persona is often seen more clearly – he may be haunted by some event in his past, or obsessed with revenge, and is often bitter and selfish, though he does undergo a change during the course of the film and redeems himself by the end.

Thus, Stewart in *Vertigo* represents the culmination of this aspect of his screen persona, the ultimate expression of Stewart as the nasty, obsessive, violent and finally, quite unsympathetic, hero. Though filmed only four years after *Rear Window*, Stewart appears to have aged noticeably – he is obviously a middle-aged man for whom the term 'mid-life crisis' is a gross understatement, infatuated with a girl half his age. (Stewart was 49 at the time, while Kim Novak was 24.)

When he behaves extremely badly (and violently) at the film's final climax, having discovered that Judy and Madeleine are the same girl, this is not really something new but merely a heightening of his already nasty behaviour. He forces her to go back with him to the bell tower, scene of the earlier crime, in the belief that a cathartic reliving of the experience can exorcize his own guilt and cure his acrophobia. He is a sick man.

Of course, Stewart gives a remarkable and convincing performance here, but was probably not aware at the time of how thoroughly Hitchcock was destroying his movie star image. As one critic has noted, 'No matter how often one sees *Vertigo*, the Stewart performance remains a surprise. Mr Stewart plays it with such deceptive common sense that the full measure of the character isn't appreciated until the final frame' which shows us the shattered shell of a man 'utterly destroyed by his own delusion'.

Not surprisingly, movie audiences at the time were baffled by the film, which was by far the least successful at the box office of the three Stewart-Hitchcock movies in the 1950s. Aside from Stewart, Barbara Bel Geddes was exactly right in the role of his supportive and wisecracking girlfriend, while Kim Novak never again had a role that suited her so perfectly. Her special blend of cool sensuality as Madeleine, and slightly vulgar charms as Judy, couldn't possibly be improved on, although she was not Hitchcock's first choice for the role. In her own way, Novak's performance is just as memorable, and contributes as much to the special qualities of the film, as that of Stewart. In the words of Samuel Taylor, 'If we'd had a brilliant actress who really created two distinctly different people, it would not have been as good. She seemed so naïve in the part, and that was good. She was always believable. There was no "art" about it, and that's why it worked so very well.'

Hitchcock's non-exclusive contract with Paramount allowed him to do occasional films for other studios. Thus, he was signed up by MGM in 1957 to do a movie adaptation of a book they owned, *The Wreck of the Mary Deare*. During the mid-1950s, the giant MGM had been experiencing serious financial difficulties. Once the biggest and most successful of the large Hollywood studios, it was now desperate to acquire the services of top independent producer-directors, such as Hitchcock.

For his scriptwriter on the project Hitchcock requested Ernest Lehman who was currently employed by the studio. Although Lehman was unenthusiastic about this particular subject, he found that he got on well with Hitchcock, who then suggested that they might do something else together instead – without bothering to inform MGM. (By the time Hitchcock met with the MGM executives to outline the story he had been developing with Lehman, they were enthusiastic, thinking they might actually get two films from him. Eventually the Mary Deare project was assigned to another writer-director team who completed the film in 1959.)

Lehman was attracted to the idea of doing 'the Hitchcock picture to end all Hitchcock pictures'. They discussed various ideas revolving around a chase theme, of a man on the run across the northern US from the United Nations headquarters in New York to Mt Rushmore National Park in South Dakota. But it all came together more clearly when Hitchcock recalled an idea that he had been offered to him by a New York newspaperman: what if the CIA had created a non-existent government agent as a decoy to divert the attention of some enemy spies away from the real agent, and the innocent hero happens to get mistaken for the decoy.

In fact, the initial work on the script took place in 1957 before Hitchcock had even begun filming *Vertigo*. This meant that Lehman had plenty of time to do background research on police and courtroom precedures and on possible settings from Long Island and New York to Chicago and South Dakota. In accordance with the director's preferred practice, he and Lehman were able to develop all their ideas fully before the start of filming in the summer of 1958. This was important, because the two men, between them, came up with so much good, new material that the project kept growing, to the point where it certainly went beyond his treatment of similar themes in any of his previous films. Though loosely related to such earlier black-and-white productions as *The 39 Steps*, *Young and Innocent* and *Saboteur*, the new film was actually Hitchcock's only original film project of the 1950s – aside from *The Man Who Knew Too Much*, based on the 1930s version of the story, which was itself a film original. However, Hitch succeeded in avoiding the weaknesses of this, his only remake, by developing an entirely fresh and new treatment. Certainly, *North by Northwest*, as the new picture would be named, benefited from the fact that it was based on a delightfully witty, inventive and lively screenplay.

The film emerged as a special production in many respects. Different in tone from the more serious pictures that Hitchcock was making during his peak creative years in the late 1950s, it marked a temporary return to a lighter, more humourous and entertaining style, full of typically 'Hitchcockian' touches and with an obvious commercial appeal, especially when cast with three leading stars: Cary Grant, Eva Marie Saint and James Mason. (It would prove to be his biggest hit since *Rear Window*.) Yet there were many opportunities for imaginative filming, too.

As his fifth VistaVision production it presents an interesting contrast with *Vertigo*. Whereas on that relatively intimate film he made special creative use of the process, here he would have a larger cast and greater variety of settings. And the broader scope of the film generally lent itself to VistaVision filming. In fact, Hitchcock specially brought the VistaVision cameras with him to MGM where it was virtually unknown, for the process was so closely linked with arch rival Paramount. (MGM's preferred process in the 1950s had been CinemaScope, which was being replaced by 35mm Panavision just around this time.)

Here Hitchcock would make the most of his last opportunity to use the process, for it was reaching the end of its life around 1958–9. The use of wide angle lenses and general sharpness of definition was ideal for filming his frightened and 'insignificant' hero on the run – dwarfed by giant buildings or observed as a tiny speck in the distance. At one point he is totally alone within a vast expanse of flat and empty prairie stretching far into the distance, suddenly finding himself under attack from the air, with nowhere to hide. He is forced to flee for his life from a small, crop-dusting airplane armed with a machine gun – one of the most celebrated and gripping set-piece sequences in the Hitchcock canon.

Representing perhaps the ultimate expression of Hitchcockian black humour and his sense of absurd, danger can appear suddenly and unexpectedly at any time or place. And his unfortunate hero has no idea what to expect next – from that point in the film when he is first mistaken for agent 'Kaplan' and is suddenly kidnapped from the crowded lobby of New York's Plaza Hotel by two polite, but tough, men in suits. He is plunged into a sequence of events that he cannot understand and over which he has no control.

Later in the film, Grant is again pursued by the same two men into a crowded lift, but his mother finds it difficult to believe his story: 'You men aren't trying to kill my son, are you?' she asks brightly. After a moment of embarrassed silence everyone laughs. He manages to escape, but soon after finds himself in deeper water than ever, implicated in a very public knife murder. There is a clear echo here of *The 39 Steps* as he is now on the run from the police, too; he manages to board the 20th Century Ltd to Chicago and meets the attractive blonde heroine for the first time. She helps him to avoid the cops, but later sets him up to be killed by the baddies instead, in an effort to protect herself (a neat reversal of the situation in *Notorious* when Cary Grant was the government agent putting *his* job first in his behaviour towards Ingrid Bergman, who is placed in great danger by trusting *him*).

In the final, climactic chase sequence hero and heroine scramble for their lives along the cliff edge, dwarfed by the giant sculpted Presidential heads on Mt Rushmore – a remarkable studio reconstruction is used here. It provides an appropriate ending to the enemy spy theme with Cold War undertones and the very American qualities of the film generally, with its range of locations and landmarks.

In fact, *North by Northwest* finally emerged as Hitchcock's longest film ever at 136 minutes. He and Lehman had succeeded in filling out

Cary Grant and Eva Marie Saint flee for their lives near the end of *North by Northwest* (1959), while the giant, impassive profile of Teddy Roosevelt provides an appropriately surreal backdrop. With the help of art director Robert Boyle, Hitch had great fun with his studio reconstruction of the giant, sculpted, Presidential heads on Mt Rushmore, featured in the climax of the film and recalling his earlier, similar use of the roof of the British Museum in *Blackmail* and the Statue of Liberty in *Saboteur* (1942).

the basic 'man on the run' theme with a much fuller development of all the leading characters. The picture certainly stands out as the very best of Cary Grant's later career. Given the opportunity to demonstrate, once again, his seemingly ageless quality, in his mid-fifties he was still able to play convincingly the debonair and romantic action hero. In marked contrast to James Stewart in *Vertigo*, who clearly looks his age, Grant here is five years older but so youthful is his image that one hardly notices, for example, that he is twenty years older than Eva Marie Saint. His mother is played by Jesse Royce Landis (previously seen in the role of Grace Kelly's extravagantly rich mother in *To Catch a Thief*). In real life she was actually a few months *younger* than Cary Grant.

Eva Marie Saint, whose special qualities as an actress were rarely appreciated in Hollywood, was here given a role that was worthy of her, as the archetypal blonde Hitchcock heroine, attractive, sophisticated, intelligent and sexy. The sexual chemistry between her and Grant is undeniable, recalling Grace Kelly and Grant in *To Catch a Thief*, as well as *Rear Window*. But she is also dangerous, as Grant learns to his cost, and resourceful enough to work undercover as a government agent. Their relationship evolves crazily during the course of the picture, complicated by deceptions and misunderstandings, but they are happily together at the final fade-out. Even a comedy-thriller benefits immensely from the fact that it is peopled by characters whom we care about, and this is one of the very best. Finally, there is James Mason at his most suave and crafty as the mastermind and leader of the spies – the most memorable Hitchcock villain since Bruno in *Strangers on a Train*. As Hitchcock later recalled, 'James Mason was the "heavy", but I didn't just want him behaving villainously. I wanted him to be polite, but not so polite that he wasn't sufficiently menacing. So I divided the character into three: gave him a secretary who *looked* menacing (Martin Landau) and a third man who was brutal' (Adam Williams).

Although *North by Northwest* was successful with the critics and the public, it failed to win any Oscars, for this was the year that MGM's epic remake of *Ben-Hur* virtually swept the board. But at least there was recognition of the film's impressive visual qualities, as with *Vertigo* the previous year. Both pictures were nominated for their art direction, which meant recognition for two of Hitchcock's favourite designers, Henry Bumstead, and Robert Boyle, whose association with the director dates back to the early 1940s (and two more productions together would follow in the early 1960s). Both Boyle and editor George Tomasini lost out to *Ben-Hur*, while a third, well deserved nomination went to Ernest Lehman for the 'story and screenplay written directly for the screen'.

At various points in his career Hitchcock worked hard planning and developing a project that he then dropped. One of the best known examples of this was in 1959, when he collaborated with writer Samuel Taylor on adapting a British novel, *No Bail for the Judge*. This Paramount project had reached a fairly advanced stage in the pre-production process when Audrey Hepburn, who had been a big Paramount star in the mid-1950s, decided she did not want to make the film. This was but one of a number of his productions that fell through around this time. His own mixed feelings about working with top stars, his anger at Audrey Hepburn in particular, his general displeasure at having to pay them what he considered to be extravagantly large fees and his own wish to vary his pictures, meant that for his next Paramount production he suddenly turned to something very different. In place of *No Bail for the Judge*, which would have been a major production filmed in London, he decided to shoot a relatively small scale black-and-white film instead, recalling his similar decision to make *The Wrong Man* a few years earlier.

It would be based on a recently published American novel, *Psycho* by Robert Bloch, and would continue his current run of American productions. (It was his British and international projects that had all fallen through.) But in most other respects the film represented a major departure for him. Loosely based on the true and extraordinary story of serial killer Edward Gein, the sheer power of the narrative, along with the unexpected shocks and violence, which were an integral part of the conception, meant that Hitchcock would be making his first *horror* thriller. The executives at Paramount were horrified. But this was the all too predictable reaction at a major Hollywood studio to what was regarded as the kind of 'exploitation' subject best left to cheap little companies like AIP in the US or Hammer Films in Britain.

Although they were not pleased about the money lost and time wasted on the abortive projects, they were even more unhappy about Hitchcock's latest idea, according to Herbert Coleman. 'They didn't like the title, the story, or anything about it at all.' However, since Hitchcock was determined to make the film, Paramount finally agreed to distribute it. He, would finance the production himself and shoot it as cheaply as possible at the Revue Studios, the television production facility at Universal where he already had his own production team turning out the episodes for his television series.

By chance, the production of *Psycho* coincided with the first stages in a takeover of the Universal studio by the giant MCA agency, which represented Hitchcock. It is quite likely that he would have been invited to move from Paramount to Universal on the completion of the deal in 1962. But his dispute with Paramount over *Psycho* and the fact that it was shot on the Universal lot, meant that he was halfway to joining Universal already.

When *Psycho* turned out to be a smash hit, of course everyone was happy. Paramount made its profits from distributing the film (though it really did not deserve them). Hitchcock received his share of the profits before exchanging the film rights and the rights to his television series for a large share in the new Universal studio. Universal not only re-released the picture but also produced the two sequels in the 1980s (*Psycho II* and *III*) a few years after Hitchcock's death, along with an unsuccessful TV movie and pilot for a possible series on television called *Bates Motel*, starring Bud Cort, in 1987. During the years since 1960,

In the opening reels of *Psycho* we are led to identify closely with the heroine, Janet Leigh, when she steals $40,000 and sets out in her car. Her long and lonely drive is brilliantly handled by Hitchcock, including a scary encounter with a highway cop, reflecting Hitch's own life-long fear of the police. Here she nervously hides the packet of money she has stolen when asked to produce her driving licence by the curious cop.

the standing set, including the motel and the gothic mansion on the hill above, became a regular tourist attraction and a feature of the Universal studio tour in Hollywood. In addition, at Universal Studios, Florida (in Orlando), newly opened for the 1990s, the interior of the Bates Motel and '*Psycho* Sound Stage' are the centrepiece of one of the featured 'audience participation' exhibits. ('Experience the art of making movies as demonstrated by Alfred Hitchcock, the master of mystery and suspense', reads the official press release. 'Universal Studios Florida reveals the terrifying secrets of the legendary director whose name sends a chill down your spine . . .') Thus, anyone could be forgiven for thinking that *Psycho* had been a Universal, not a Paramount, production.

For Hitchcock, *Psycho* would mark a kind of culminating point in his later career. As by far his biggest and most profitable hit, it would make him extremely wealthy and confirm his reputation as one of the most commercially successful American directors of the postwar era. *Psycho* was the first of his later films in which he would use a younger generation of actors and generally avoid the very top stars, who also demanded the highest fees, in contrast to his practice during the 1940s and 1950s. In addition, *Psycho* brought to an end that regular pattern of directing at least one feature per year which he had maintained, virtually without a break, since the beginning of his career. There would be a two-year gap between *Psycho* and *The Birds*, and after *Marnie*, in 1964, the gaps between pictures would get even longer. It is appropriate, too, that *Psycho* would be his last in black-and-white – his last, notable contribution to an aesthetic tradition that he had done so much to enrich during the course of his long career. It emerged as one of his very darkest works, the ultimate expression of Hitchcockian black humour, and fullest exploration of the theme of the psychotic murderer. Thus, it appears to bring his career full circle, for there are clear thematic links with his first notable successes in the 1920s such as *The Lodger* and *Blackmail*. *Psycho* represented Hitchcock's last, powerful and stylized use of black-and-white at a time when the long tradition of black-and-white filming was winding down generally in the US and England, just before the change-over to colour. (After 1966, relatively few American feature films were made in black and white). Hitch was but one of a number of directors – including Samuel Fuller, John Frankenheimer (with *The Manchurian Candidate*) Stanley Kubrick, with *Dr Strangelove* and Roman Polanski with *Repulsion*, itself a spinoff of *Psycho* – who were reminding movie audiences just how effective black-and-white could be. (As he himself explained to one of his assistants early on in the filming, 'It will have so much more *impact* in black-and-white'.)

Of the two black-and-white pictures filmed during Hitchcock's Paramount years, one was shot at Warners and the second at Universal – both studios that were readily associated with relatively low-keyed and low cost thrillers and horror films, and with black-and-white film-making in Hollywood generally. Even during the late 1950s Universal had continued to turn out black-and-white 'B' pictures on small budgets side by side with its costlier colour productions. Thus, one of the key members of Hitchcock's crew was art director Robert Clatworthy whose experience at Universal made him a natural choice for the job. His recent credits ranged from *Written on the Wind*, in colour, and Orson Welles' *Touch of Evil*, in black-and-white, to such horror and fantasy titles as *The Incredible Shrinking Man*, *Deadly Mantis*, *Curse of the Undead* and *The Leech Woman*. (He had even worked on two Hitchcock films back in 1942 as an assistant to Robert Boyle.)

Some critics writing about *Psycho* have asserted that he used the crew from his TV series to shoot the picture quickly and cheaply. But this is not strictly true. The only important member of his television crew was cameraman John Russell, in place of Robert Burks. Otherwise his team included such regular collaborators as composer Bernard Herrmann, editor George Tomasini and Saul Bass, all of whom made special contributions, along with art directors Joseph Hurley and especially Robert Clatworthy. With his experience of black-and-white and tight budgets and familiarity with the Universal back lot, he succeeded in cannibalizing sections of existing sets and helped to keep the costs down. The designs for the Bates' house and motel were simple but effective. The standing sets were re-used in the sequels and survive on the Universal lot as a strange kind of monument to the memory of Hitchcock, while occupying a permanent place in the iconography of the American cinema. Completed at a cost of only slightly over $800,000, *Psycho* was both the most economical of all Hitchcock's American productions (if a slight adjustment is made for inflation) and his biggest ever hit. He would receive a cheque from Paramount towards the end of 1960 for $2.5 million as payment for his share of the first quarter's returns. Rentals in the US alone would total about $9 million and most of this amount was clear profit, to be divided between him and Paramount.

It is surprising to discover just how faithful Hitchcock has been to the original Robert Bloch novel, which also supplied the picture with its excellent title. In his previous screen adaptations (in the 1950s), Hitchcock generally took only those sections of the original that specially interested him and discarded the rest. But in the case of *Psycho*, he recognized the cinematic potential of the book as it existed. The main changes he made (in collaboration with scriptwriter Joseph Stefano) were in the age and appearance of the Norman Bates character, played by Anthony Perkins as a younger and more appealing figure. Similarly, the opening scenes are more fully developed to give greater prominence to the Janet Leigh role. Whereas in the novel the description of the events leading up to her arrival at the motel are told in flashback, in the film the same events, such as her decision to steal the money, her journey and exchange of cars to cover her trail, are all shown in greater detail and in the correct chronological order. Hitchcock's special twist was to create a strong audience identification with her character before killing her off.

In fact, all the main characters and scenes can be found in the original book, including the shower murder, the encounter between Norman Bates and the detective Arbogast investigating Marion's (Janet Leigh's) disappearance, also his subsequent murder by 'mother' in the Bates house behind the motel and the final climax in the fruit cellar when Lila, the sister, played by Vera Miles, is attacked by the 'old lady'. Even the final images of the dual personality Norman/mother in jail giving voice to his/her internal monologue can be found in Bloch's novel, concluding with the words, 'Why, she wouldn't even harm a fly . . .' the very same final line of both book and film. However, in each case Hitchcock's approach gives a new power and substance to the generally understated descriptions found in the book, bringing the printed pages dramatically to life on the movie screen.

The only really new scene comes at the very opening of the picture when we see Janet Leigh using her lunch break for a brief hour or so of love-making in a hotel room with her dull but handsome boyfriend played by John Gavin. This follows immediately after the strong, black-and-white graphic qualities of Saul Bass's titles and the insistent rhythms of Bernard Herrmann's score have set the tone of the drama to come. By using large numbers of close-ups of Janet Leigh in all the opening scenes, along with shots from her point of view, Hitchcock succeeds in establishing a close audience identification with her character. For example, back in her own apartment and packing to leave, she keeps glancing at the packet of stolen cash lying on her bed and Hitchcock insisted on repeatedly cutting back to shots of the money from her point of view. ('I always want the audience to think what she's thinking.')

In addition, the opening reels demonstrate the sheer power of black-and-white imagery and editing even before we get to the famous shower murder, which represents perhaps the ultimate expression of stylized violence, combining sound, music and fast editing of shots filmed from many different angles. For example, there is a memorable sequence on the road when she is followed and observed by a policeman in a patrol car who appears a bit sinister in close-up, wearing sun-glasses, when he questions her briefly.

The film turns darker when the Bates Motel looms up, dreamlike, in the distance, through the driving rain, as she is looking for a place to spend her second night on the road. There is a warmth in her briefly shared conversations and sandwiches with the young Perkins, in contrast to the relative coldness of all that has gone before. She appears to have changed her mind and decided to go back and return the money she has stolen. Thus, the shower murder by the crazy mother comes as a terrible and unexpected shock. However, Hitchcock made a special effort to present Perkins as a sympathetic character. Thus, we are led to identify with him as we observe him scrupulously cleaning up Janet Leigh's room and disposing of her car to remove all evidence of her having been there – in order to protect his mother. (From this point on we continue to identify with Perkins and his guilty secret.)

It may not be too difficult for film audiences to adjust to this sudden change of focus. But, unfortunately, there are only a few key sequences in the remainder of the film that come near to matching the sheer brilliance of the opening reels. The first hour or so of *Psycho* is such a remarkable achievement – as powerful, concise and effective a slice of cinema as has ever been accomplished on the movie screen – that the later reels must come as a bit of a letdown. Admittedly, there are some remarkable individual scenes: a memorable encounter between Martin Balsam and Perkins, who becomes progressively more tongue-tied as he tries to fend off some persistent questioning by the shrewd private detective; the staging of Balsam's murder, and the final, chilling climax in the Bates mansion, a variation on the familiar theme of the heroine in distress, when Vera Miles discovers the grisly secret. Although Perkins gives a superb performance, and has been closely identified with this role ever since, John Gavin is a colourless hero, while Vera Miles is no more than adequate as the dead girl's sister who sets out to solve the mystery of her disappearance.

Throughout the picture, Hitchcock draws on a wide range of cinematic techniques. Not only a remarkable score, editing and photography, but also a variety of special effects were used. The identity of 'mother', for example, was disguised by using a stand-in and a specially fabricated soundtrack at various points including fragments of overheard conversations, with her voice supplied by a number of different actors.

Although the film failed to win any Oscars, there were nominations for Janet Leigh's finely judged performance (as supporting actress), for black-and-white cinematography and art direction and for Hitchcock as director. But the most obvious omission was the failure of the Academy to recognize the quality and sheer originality of Bernard Herrmann's economical score: 'In using only strings, I felt that I was able to complement the black-and-white photography with a black-and-white sound.' (Surprisingly enough, Herrmann was never nominated for any of his Hitchcock scores and actually failed to receive a single nomination for thirty years, from 1946 to 1976.)

In later years, Hitchcock complained about the way in which the critics had responded to his films, in general, and to *Psycho* in particular:

> I remember the terrible panning we got when *Psycho* opened. It was a critical disaster. One critic [Bosley Crowther in the *New York Times*] called it 'a blot on an honourable career', and a couple of years later he reviewed Polanski's *Repulsion* by saying it was 'a psychological thriller in the classic style of Hitchcock's *Psycho*'. My films went from being failures to masterpieces without ever being successes . . .

Yet it was during the 1960s that attitudes towards the cinema were changing. There was, for example, a rapid growth in university film courses and in the numbers of books and magazines on the cinema. And there was a new willingness to treat Hitchcock and his films with greater respect than ever before. (Hitchcock was one of the most highly-rated directors in the pages of *Movie* magazine, published in the early 1960s, while the first books on Hitchcock in English were Peter Bogdanovich's *The Cinema of Alfred Hitchcock* in 1963 and Robin Wood's *Hitchcock's Films* in 1965.)

Yet *Psycho* was quite different from his other films. In the words of scriptwriter Joseph Stefano, 'It lacks everything predictable in Hitchcock up to that time . . . He had reached a point in his professional life when he was ready for a totally different kind of picture.' More explicit in its treatment of sex, both normal and abnormal, and with a more graphic depiction of violence, Hitchcock also took pleasure in outwitting the representatives of the Hays office who administered the film industry's self-censorship code. (He specially included a few expendable lines of dialogue and other bits that he knew they would take exception to, in order to distract them from the more essential and more subtle elements in the bizarre story, such as its perverted view of mother love. And when they had difficulty in deciding whether there was a quick bit of unacceptable nudity in the shower murder scene, he merely resubmitted it *in identical form* and got their approval second time around.) In pushing the Code as far as possible he was thus accurately anticipating and perhaps helping to precipitate changes in audience tastes in the 1960s and in American society itself, which was becoming more violent and insecure. This would be reflected in the movies and television, especially after the abandonment of the Code in favour of a new system of movie classification.

In fact, the film itself, the treatment of the psychopathic central character and especially the murder in the shower, had a great influence on the many thrillers and horror movies that followed in the 1960s and 1970s. It was a most original touch for 1960 for Hitch to present Norman Bates as a sympathetic, appealing and 'normal' looking figure within an ordinary, American, contemporary setting – nothing more ordinary and American than a roadside motel – rather than as a more obviously deranged character conforming to the conventions of the traditional horror movie, of mad scientists, haunted houses or period settings.

Psycho's influence can be seen on a wide range of directors – established figures, from Robert Aldrich in the 1960s (*Whatever Happened to Baby Jane?*, *Hush, Hush, Sweet Charlotte*) to Stanley Kubrick's *The Shining* (1980), especially a new generation of younger men including

Polanski, Brian De Palma, John Carpenter and David Cronenberg, among others. Ironically, whereas *Psycho* was filmed in black-and-white and within the restrictions of the Hays Code, most of the movies it influenced were produced in colour during the post-Code era, more shocking and gory than artistic, and lacking that special stylized power that Hitchcock achieved with his own last venture into black-and-white.

After the tremendous box-office success of *Psycho*, Hitchcock was once again faced with the problem of what kind of film to do next. Among a number of possible projects that he was considering around this time, he had bought the rights to the novel *Marnie* by Winston Graham. He hoped to interest Grace Kelly in returning to the screen, after a gap of many years, to play the lead role of an insecure lady thief. But he was also attracted to the idea of a movie based on the Daphne du Maurier story, 'The Birds'.

When Grace Kelly decided to pull out of the Marnie project, Hitchcock decided to look for another, less well known actress to play the role and spotted an attractive blonde model, Tippi Hedren, in a television advert who appealed to him. Although she had only worked previously as a model and had no real acting experience, he soon signed her to a contract. It wasn't long before he had decided to cast her as the star of his current project, *The Birds*, with *Marnie* to follow soon after.

This would mark the last time in his career that Hitchcock would direct two feature films in quick succession. In spite of the long time gap between *Psycho* and *The Birds*, he was able to reassemble virtually his entire team of favourite collaborators for these two projects, along with a new writer, Evan Hunter, with whom he got on quite well. (Although Hunter was meant to script both films, at some point Hitch decided that he preferred to have a woman scriptwriter and hired Jay Presson Allen to replace him on *Marnie*.)

Since Daphne du Maurier's 'The Birds' was little more than a long short story, set in Cornwall, it merely provided the basic idea, of unexplained bird attacks, and the title, for the movie version, which was virtually a film original. Not only were the characters and situations created afresh by Hunter and Hitchcock, but they could also develop the leading female role with a particular actress, Hedren, in mind, as Hitch had done previously with Grace Kelly in *Rear Window*. However, in spite of all the care that Hitchcock devoted to her, the inexperienced Hedren could not begin to carry the film on her own, and her co-star, the Australian actor Rod Taylor, though a reasonably competent actor was no Cary Grant. Yet the weaknesses of some of the performances and scripting were more than made up for by the film's remarkable special effects and apocalyptic vision, especially in the second half.

Psycho **Budget Breakdown on selective costs ($) (1959–60)**

Director's fee (Hitchcock–deferred)		$250,000
Script and book		
Rights to Bloch novel	9,000	
First script (James P. Cavanaugh)	7,166	
Second/final script (Stefano)	17,500	33,666
Stars and leading cast		
Anthony Perkins	40,000	
Janet Leigh	25,000	
John Gavin (6 weeks @ 5,000)	30,000	
Vera Miles (1,750 per week)	10,000 (est.)	
Patricia Hitchcock (2 days @ 500)	1,000	
John McIntire & Laurene Tuttle	1,250	
other cast, misc.	2,750	110,000
Sets design and construction		
Bates motel and house exterior	15,000	
„ „ interiors	6,000	
Basement and fruit cellar	2,500	
Mother's bedroom	1,250	
Loomis hardware store in Fairvale	3,000	
Fairvale County courthouse interiors	2,000	29,750
Editor – George Tomasini (26 weeks @ 425)		11,000
Composer – Bernard Herrmann (double original agreed minimum fee of 17,500)		34,501
Pictorial consultant – Saul Bass		
general fee	10,000	
shower scene storyboards	2,000	12,000
Title sequence		
Saul Bass fee	3,000	
other (production) costs	21,000	24,000
Make-up and hairdressing		300
		$505,217
Other costs (film stock, cameras, studio overhead, etc.)		301,730
		Total $806,448.

Principal filming at Universal Studios, Hollywood 30 November 1959 to 1 February 1960

Source: Stephen Rebello, *Alfred Hitchcock and the Making of Psycho* (Dembner Books, New York, 1990)

In the opening reels the tone is generally light and romantic as socialite Tippi Hedren first meets lawyer Rod Taylor in a San Francisco pet shop. There is a good-natured interplay between them, one practical joke leads to another, and in order to deliver a surprise gift, undetected, the following day, she drives to his mother's home in Bodega Bay, seventy miles north of the city. Here the rest of the film takes place, during the course of one long weekend.

Hitchcock is absolutely precise about the time scale involved, showing the escalation of events during a relatively short period of time. Much of the picture is shot on location, making effective use of the geography of the town and the Brenner family home across the bay. Thus, Hedren's practical joke initially involves her in hiring a boat, and it is on her return journey that she is suddenly attacked by a seagull for no apparent reason. Although another gull smashes into the door later that evening, it is only on the following day that the situation begins to look more serious, when a flock of hostile gulls disrupt a children's outdoor party. That evening hundreds of finches invade the house by swooping down the chimney. Finally, the bird attacks escalate out of control during the course of the long and climactic third day.

Hitchcock initially presents us with a fairly conventional view of the characters and setting – attractive blonde, eligible young bachelor son, possessive mother (Jessica Tandy), a sympathetic ex-girlfriend who is the local schoolteacher (Suzanne Pleshette), and a younger sister. Returning to colour and a standard wide-screen format (with his favoured Vista-Vision system no longer available), the predominantly soft colour tonality of the film is reflected in the appearance of the cool-looking blonde heroine in her stylish light green suit. He generally avoids strong colours, though a bright red recurs at various points – associated with the schoolteacher who is killed by the birds, and with the fleeing school-children at the outdoor party.

Having taken on many different technical challenges during the course of his long career, Hitchcock had never ventured into the science fiction or fantasy genre before, nor made a film that relied so heavily on a wide range of special effects. In fact, the picture also qualifies as a kind of 'disaster movie', related to the many, generally cheaply made apocalyptic movies of the era (in black-and-white) such as *The World, the Flesh and the Devil* (1959), *The Day the Earth Caught Fire* (1961) and *Panic in Year Zero* (1962).

The variety and scope of the bird attacks in the second half were matched by the variety of visual effects, including matte painting, travelling mattes, and rotoscoping, along with mechanical models, occasionally used within the same shot along with trained, live birds and the

Hitchcock rehearses actor Rod Taylor on location in Northern California for one of the key scenes in *The Birds* (1963) when Taylor and Tippi Hedren find that their friend (Suzanne Pleshette) is one of the first victims of the savage and unexplained bird attacks. In this picture the human characters were overshadowed by the remarkable (Oscar-nominated) special visual effects. Though Hitch's films were generally known for their technical excellence, this was the last time that he would receive a nomination from the Academy.

actors. This meant that in addition to his normal production crew, Hitch-cock hired an entire team of special effects experts headed by Ub Iwerks, Albert Whitlock and Lawrence A. Hampton, with specialist bird trainer Ray Berwick, while composer Bernard Herrmann worked with Remi Gassmann and Oskar Sala to produce an original and appropriate 'score' that depended entirely on a blend of bird sounds and electronic sound effects.

near Bodega School.

437 Melanie - Run - Run.

440 Children (foregrnd against Sodium Screen) Backgrnd
Bodega school with michelle and 2 or 3 children

440A continuation of 440 - Melanie runs past camera

The most striking image of all is a bird's eye view from high above the town, including a pair of gulls who drop into shot from each side of the frame. As one critic noted, 'the town as seen in the overhead shot does not actually exist. It was an Albert Whitlock matte painting, into which a backlot fire was inserted, filmed from a hill overlooking the Universal car park. The gulls were filmed from a clifftop on the island of Santa Cruz, west of Los Angeles, and rotoscoped into the shot. Making the mattes for this alone took two artists three months, for a shot lasting less than twenty seconds.' (Rotoscoping is a form of animation, making use of careful tracing of a photographed image, by hand, while the travelling matte is a sophisticated form of double exposure.)

Similarly, at the end of the film the birds appear to have taken over the area entirely, though they allow the family to escape in their car to an uncertain future. The final shot, in which the entire landscape, as far as the eye can see, is dominated by thousands of birds – the car seen travelling along the road and disappearing into the distance – is a single, elaborate, composite (multiple exposure) shot made up of thirty different elements. Here Hitchcock brilliantly provides a suitably unusual and open-ended conclusion to the film: all the people are gone, leaving nature triumphant, and the silence is only broken by the occasional sound of chirping birds and the rustling of wings.

The picture also provided plenty of opportunity for Hitchcockian black humour, such as the tense moment when the heroine arrives outside the local school and sees a few birds perched innocently on the jungle gym in the playground. A minute later Hitch cuts back to the same shot and we/she see that the jungle gym is now packed tightly with hundreds of birds, which seem to have suddenly materialized out of nowhere, with no warning, and are ready to attack.

In fact, *The Birds* proved to be such an unusual undertaking for the director that he found himself making some changes during the course of filming, improvising some new bits of action on the set and introducing

This series of continuity sketches (or storyboard) by art director Robert Boyle gives some idea of the way in which one of the most gripping and effective sequences in *The Birds* was first planned out by Hitchcock and his production team. Here Melanie, played by Tippi Hedren, and a group of children are suddenly attacked by the birds outside the Bodega school. One of the many complicated special effects sequences, the human figures are photographed first, then the birds added separately making use of a background matte and rotoscoping (a frame by frame animation technique).

additional close-ups of Tippi Hedren to involve the audience more closely in the action from her point of view. As he told François Truffaut:

> Something happened that was altogether new in my experience. I began to study the scenario as we went along, and I saw that there were weaknesses in it . . . [Thus,] I began to improvise. For instance, the whole scene of the (outside) attack on the house by birds that are not seen was done spontaneously, right on the set. I'd almost never done anything like that before, but I made up my mind and quickly designed the movements of the people. I decided that the mother and the little girl would dart around to search for shelter. There was no place to run for cover, so I made them move about in contradictory directions, a little like rats scurrying into corners. I deliberately shot Melanie Daniels [Hedren] from a distance because I wanted to make it clear that she was recoiling from nothing at all . . . [But] the whole scene that follows is a transfer from the objective viewpoint to the subjective view . . . The reverse cuts of Melanie, as she looks at the mother going back and forth, subtly indicate what she's thinking. Her eyes and gestures indicate an increasing concern over the mother's strange behaviour and for the mother herself. The vision of the reality belongs to the girl . . .

Finally, there was the horrific and climactic attack on the heroine who is trapped in the upstairs attic. This was one sequence that could not be accomplished convincingly with the use of special effects, and Tippi Hedren was forced to endure a week of sheer hell as live birds were thrown at her, and even attached to her clothing by elastic bands so that they would not fly away too quickly. Each time the cameras stopped, 'a new setup was arranged, her clothing was torn slightly and stage blood painted on, the make-up for a scratch was applied by artist Howard Smits, her hair was disarrayed a little more – and the ordeal continued.' As recalled by fellow actress Jessica Tandy, 'Day after day, for an entire week, the poor woman put up with that. She was alone in that caged room, acting, with the birds coming at her, and with costume changes and make-up applications and all the stage blood, she couldn't even go to the commissary for lunch . . . and I just don't know how she did it.' Perhaps Hitchcock went a bit too far this time in order to achieve the effects he required; it is the real, frightened responses of the actress that we see up on the screen.

Although *The Birds* did reasonably well at the box office, it had been an expensive and time-consuming film to make. Principal photography was completed by the beginning of July 1962, but Hitchcock then spent an additional six months on the editing and getting the special effects just right. Thus, the completed picture was not ready for release until early in 1963 – leading some writers to conclude that there had been a three-year, rather than a two-year, gap between *Psycho* and *The Birds*. The film only earned a small profit and was nominated for but one Oscar, for special visual effects, on the whole, a disappointing result for the first picture delivered under his new Universal contract. There would be worse to come. Two of his next three features would flop badly. *Marnie*, his next production, budgeted at $2 million, about half the cost of *The Birds*, would just about break even – his worst result since *The Wrong Man*, eight years earlier. However, with *Torn Curtain* (1966) and *Topaz* (1969) he returned to the $4–5 million cost range. If the earlier film broke even, representing yet another disappointing result, *Topaz* was an outright disaster, probably the worst flop of his career. At least for his last two films, in the 1970s, he was careful to keep the costs down, and a modest return to form meant that he was able to end his movie-making career on a moderately successful note. Whereas four of his six Paramount productions had done quite well at the box office, including one big hit (*Rear Window*) along with the phenomenally successful *Psycho*, not one of his six for Universal would do really well, which meant that the profits for the entire group would be tiny. (One of Hitch's regular camera assistants has suggested that he was happier, and was treated better, at Paramount; but the fact is that during the Paramount period he was at his peak, while he was older and less sure of himself during the Universal years, thus it is not surprising that he was treated accordingly.)

Hitchcock had played an important role in the careers of many of his female stars in particular, beginning with Joan Fontaine and Ingrid Bergman in the 1940s, had perhaps his biggest success with Grace Kelly in the 1950s and did less well with Vera Miles, who was under contract to him for a number of years. But never before had he attempted to take a virtual unknown, a model who had never acted before and turn her into a movie star. Although Tippi Hedren had appreciated his efforts at first, she suffered quite a traumatic experience in filming *The Birds* and was unhappy at Hitchcock's efforts to control her personal life as well. In fact, relations between them soured during filming of *Marnie*, their second (and last) film together. According to writer Donald Spoto, this dispute with Hedren caused Hitchcock to lose all interest in the picture, midway through production: 'Hitchcock seemed to want *Marnie* to fail, in fact, and he no longer took any concern even for the technical details, the special effects, or the careful use of rear projection and artificial sets that, with much hesitation, had been planned for major scenes.' And if this quite extraordinary and unsubstantiated statement is not sufficient, he goes on to refer to the film's 'glaring technical blunders', an interesting example of his tendency to confuse his critical response to the final film, which he had himself referred to only a few years earlier as 'one of Hitchcock's dozen great works', with his attempted 'exposé' of Hitchcock's private life.

In fact, *Marnie* is a remarkable and memorable picture that benefits from repeated viewing, like all of Hitchcock's best works. After the 'one-off' experiments of *Psycho* and *The Birds*, *Marnie* represented a return to more familiar and more personal, Hitchcockian territory. The film is in the tradition of classic Hitchcock productions from *Spellbound* and *Notorious* to *Vertigo*, while the mid-Atlantic East Coast settings clearly recall *Strangers on a Train*. And the central relationship in *To Catch a Thief*, of a beautiful, rich girl attracted to a handsome gentleman thief, was here neatly reversed: in *Marnie* it is the gent who is attracted to the blonde lady thief, while the triangle situation that develops with his more conventional (and jealous) former girlfriend resembles that in *Vertigo*. (Diane Baker gives a memorable performance here in the difficult role of the other woman.)

For the leading role of Mark, Hitchcock surprisingly chose Sean Connery, fresh from his early success as James Bond. (*Marnie* was shot in between *From Russia with Love* and *Goldfinger*, the second and third Bond films respectively.) A convincing looking man of action who could also be sensitive and caring, in the Cary Grant tradition, Connery here gives an excellent performance, fully justifying Hitchcock's confidence in him. This was really his first opportunity to demonstrate his range and qualities as an actor, and Hitchcock must be credited with being one of the first directors to recognize his potential.

Yet he is hardly a conventional hero character – a former zoologist who is initially fascinated and intrigued by Marnie before he falls in love and virtually forces her to marry him. He stalks and captures her like a big game hunter. ('I'm just something you've caught. You think I'm some kind of animal you've trapped.') He can be sadistic and cruel, and there is something a bit kinky about his attraction to her in the first place, while Hitch also makes special use of Connery's ability to project a certain insolent rebelliousness and stubbornness, too.

He is well matched by Tippi Hedren, quite convincing in the difficult role of the deeply disturbed and frigid heroine whose only real love is her favourite horse, Forio. Hitchcock's stylized treatment of the riding sequences, with back projection, gives these scenes a slightly unreal quality, while her irrational reactions to the colour red, conveyed at various points through the use of a red filter, appears to have annoyed some critics (such as Spoto). In addition, there is the fantasy world of Baltimore (where her mother still lives), of Marnie's disturbed childhood memories, presented in flashback. In the Baltimore scenes, Hitchcock

Hitchcock's qualities as a fine and sensitive director of actors were often overlooked by the critics, who tended to concentrate more on the familiar action and suspense sequences in his films. Here he is seen instructing the three young stars of *Marnie* (1964) in a key bedroom sequence when Marnie (Tippi Hedren) wakes from a nightmare and is forced to recognize the extent of her mental illness. (Left to right): Tippi Hedren, Diane Baker, Hitch and Sean Connery.

makes effective use of an expressionistic looking street set, dominated by a giant ship. He had often utilized such techniques in his earlier, black-and-white films, such as *Spellbound*, with its dream and flashback sequences, and there were many back projection shots in *Notorious*. But perhaps it is the otherwise more 'naturalistic' qualities of colour filming that make it difficult for some critics to accept. (Though it must be admitted that there are a few surprising examples of badly done process shots and sloppy editing.) As with *The Birds* before it and *Torn Curtain* which followed, *Marnie* was filmed in the relatively soft and cool colours most favoured by Hitchcock, making his use of red filters at various points appear even more jarringly dramatic.

In addition, some writers have criticized the film for its amateur psychologizing, but there is no suggestion of a simple cure for Marnie's neuroses. By the end of the picture, Mark has merely succeeded in breaking through her defences and gained some recognition of her problems and a new willingness on her part to seek help. The film builds up a powerful momentum in the second half that is finally resolved during the course of one long climactic day, including the death of her favourite horse and ending with a visit to her mother and her house on that strange looking street.

Marnie, like virtually all of Hitchcock's pictures, was carefully planned out in advance. Transcripts exist of tapes of some of the early pre-production conferences, which make it clear that the kind of techniques used by him were an integral part of his approach to the subject and not merely some hastily devised afterthought. One of the most sadly under-rated of all his films, it marked a fitting conclusion to his most creative years. And just as this, his most remarkable period, began with the under-appreciated low-keyed drama, *The Wrong Man*, it was only to be expected that *Marnie*, a complex and unconventional treatment of a dark and difficult subject, would fail to appeal to movie audiences at the time, recalling his similarly disappointing experience with *Vertigo* a few years earlier.

After such a memorable and varied run of pictures, and having set such a high standard during these late, peak years of his career, it was almost inevitable that those that followed would look relatively disappointing and that his skills as a film-maker would decline as he grew older. The only question was at what point this would begin to happen. It could not have been easy for him to carry on in later years knowing how really impossible it would be to continue to maintain the same quality while appealing to a new, younger generation of movie-goers.

8

1965-76: Hitchcock in Decline

From *Torn Curtain* to *Family Plot*

Depressed by the failure of *Marnie* at the box office (and with the critics), and perhaps beginning to show his age, Hitchcock found it more difficult than ever to select a subject for his next film. There was a gap of about two years before he began shooting his next feature, *Torn Curtain*, towards the end of 1965. A relatively rare example of a Hitchcock film based on an original story and screenplay, it was credited to Ulster writer Brian Moore, but he insists that much of the final script was written by Hitchcock himself, although other writers also contributed.

In any case, some of the most obvious weaknesses in the final film can be traced back to the script and an extremely unconvincing portrait of East Germany during the Cold War era where much of the film is supposed to take place. And surely no one in the movie audience is taken in by the situation as it develops early on, in which the nuclear scientist hero (Paul Newman) is seen 'defecting' to the Communists, while there is a similar failure to involve the viewer with the plight of his fiancée (Julie Andrews). She observes his strange and unexplained behaviour and even follows him on his flight behind the Iron Curtain.

Both of the picture's stars look ill at ease in their roles. Hitchcock apparently did not get on well with either of them and even claimed that Andrews was virtually forced on him by the studio, since she was regarded as a tremendous box office draw at the time, fresh from her success in *The Sound of Music*. (The executives at Universal may have also recalled that Hitchcock got a fine performance from another singer, Doris Day, in *The Man Who Knew Too Much* a few years earlier.)

In addition, Hitchcock resented paying their extremely high fees, accounting for 20 per cent of the budget, although this was probably balanced out to some extent at the box office, for the completed film did reasonably well and earned a small profit in spite of its relatively high cost. But other costs were kept under control by shooting much of the picture in the studio and using few locations, mainly in nearby California, such as the University of Southern California (USC) campus and a farm in Camarillo.

However, in spite of the fact that the director was working with a mainly new production team combining British and American collaborators, the film looks unmistakably a Hitchcock production. Most notable of all is the 'desaturated' and controlled use of colour, a further extension of the kind of restrained tonal range previously favoured by him on such films as *The Birds* and *Marnie*. (It is worth noting that he was able to get such excellent results even with a less well-known cameraman, John F. Warren, who had filmed two of his television episodes; though some writers have stated that Hitch was forced to find a new lighting cameraman due to the death of Robert Burks in a fire, in fact Burks' death in 1968 came long after shooting was completed, so there must be some other explanation for the director's decision to drop him from this film.) But, unfortunately, Hitchcock had a falling out with Bernard Herrmann over his score and turned to British composer John Addison instead, while editor George Tomasini had died shortly after *Marnie* was completed, forcing Hitchcock to find a new editor, too.

If the picture is less than vintage Hitchcock, it does still include a familiar mix of suspense and action, and characteristically wicked black humour. For example, Gromek, the security officer and the most sinister character in the film, is given a certain offbeat appeal by the fact that he is so eager to make small talk, proudly demonstrating his knowledge of American slang and frequently reminiscing about the time when he lived in New York City. Thus, one cannot help feeling a little sorry for him when he is subjected to a particularly gruesome death.

In fact, *Torn Curtain* is most often remembered for its nasty and prolonged murder sequence; blending Hitchcockian black humour with genuine violence in about equal proportions, it purports to show how difficult and messy it can be to kill someone on the spur of the moment using whatever weapons are to hand. But perhaps it goes on a bit too long, as if Hitch was not merely content to make his point. For not only did he force the actors to go on and on, in filming the scene, but also he appears to want the movie audience to squirm and feel uncomfortable, too. (This scene recalls the horrific bird attacks on Tippi Hedren in the climax to *The Birds*.)

If *Torn Curtain* suffers most from Hitchcock's surprising failure, at the most basic level, to involve the movie audiences with his characters, and added little to his reputation as a director, *Topaz*, his next film, turned out to be a far more seriously flawed work. Instead of following *Torn*

Curtain by trying something new and different and more personal, as he undoubtedly would have done during his peak years, it was an indication of the continuing decline in his creative powers that he chose to do yet another international spy thriller with a Cold War theme at this time, virtually admitting that he had nothing new to offer. (On *Topaz*, Hitchcock truly ventured into the world of international production, so very characteristic of the 1960s, when the American studios were financing many such productions – *Torn Curtain* only *appeared* to be international in scope, and was in fact filmed mainly in California.)

He who had been so influential in the past, establishing trends for other directors to follow, was apparently now content merely to follow 60s trends. Since *Topaz* was based on a popular bestseller by Leon Uris, a fictitious treatment of the 1962 Cuban missile crisis, it appeared to represent a fairly safe choice of subject. Yet there had been so many spy thrillers done during the 1960s, especially large numbers of imitations of the popular James Bond cycle and often making use of a variety of foreign locations, that movie audiences had suffered from a surfeit of such films. Thus, there was a danger that even such an apparently 'safe' subject could flop at the box office if Hitchcock failed to deliver something exceptional.

In fact, he took a risk in not including any big stars among his cast, which mixed American, Canadian and especially French actors. And he opted for a virtually unknown leading man, Frederick Stafford, who had previously played the role of secret agent OSS 117, one of the many James Bond imitations filmed in France in the mid-1960s. Although Hitchcock would save money on the actors, the picture would require some expensive location filming (in Copenhagen, New York and Paris), so it would not be cheap to produce. In addition, the mainly American production team would include a British cameraman (Jack Hildyard) and a leading French composer of film music (Maurice Jarre) who would contribute to the international flavour of the production.

Considering that the gaps between Hitchcock's films were getting longer, this might suggest that he would be better prepared for filming. But, in the case of *Topaz* he was not ready at all and the production was in trouble from the very start. The script provided by Leon Uris was totally unsuitable. Yet Hitchcock was already committed to production dates that could not be changed. Although he managed to get his writer friend Samuel Taylor to fly over to join him in London at short notice, a completed script obviously could not be ready in time. As Taylor later recalled, '*Topaz* was a dreadful experience, because Hitchcock . . . had me writing scenes a few days – and in many cases a few hours – before they were shot. It was very difficult for all of us . . .'

At least the picture starts off well, with a characteristically gripping set-piece sequence set in Copenhagen and showing a Russian defector and his family evading Russian agents and escaping safely to the West. And later on, the death of the Cuban spy mistress (Karen Dor) is quite stunning: filmed from overhead, her purple dress spreads out like a flower opening as she collapses onto the floor. But a clear indication of Hitchcock's unhappiness with the film was his problem in making a choice between three different endings.

Hurriedly scripted and poorly acted, *Topaz* emerged as the biggest disaster of his American career, an unqualified flop with film critics and audiences alike. Yet he had obviously made an effort to appeal to modern moviegoers. Pauline Kael is wrong to assert that '*Topaz* (is) the same damned spy picture he's been making since the thirties, and it's getting longer, slower and duller.' For *Topaz* is bad in a new and different way. Clearly Hitch had lost touch with his audience and appeared no longer capable of saying anything new.

Such a loss-maker could not have come at a worse time for his studio, Universal, which had experienced a drastic fall in profits in 1969 – one of the many Hollywood companies suffering from a dreadful slump at the box office. (20th Century-Fox, MGM and Warners all recorded large losses that same year.) However, for Hitchcock, after the failure of *Topaz*, things could only get better. In fact, he had a modest success with his last two features in the 1970s, *Frenzy* and *Family Plot*. By this time he was in his seventies and the best that could be expected of him was a flair for reworking some of his most familiar and favourite themes. By keeping costs low his films could still earn a reasonable profit. Both pictures were received respectfully, rather than enthusiastically, by the press as representing something of a modest return to form.

With *Frenzy* in 1971, Hitchcock returned to British production for the first time since *Stage Fright* over twenty years earlier (though parts of *The Man Who Knew Too Much* had been filmed in London in 1956). Although Universal, along with the other Hollywood studios, had closed its production office in London a year or two earlier when British films· had 'gone out of fashion', there was no objection to Hitchcock returning on his own, especially as this meant that his new picture could be produced for half the cost of *Topaz*.

Hitchcock had been attracted to Arthur La Bern's novel *Goodbye Piccadilly, Farewell Leicester Square*, which he regarded merely as a useful point of departure. Hitchcock got on well with English writer Anthony Shaffer, who later remarked on the director's special interest in 'bizarre sexual crimes'. Certainly the film includes one rather horrific rape and strangling sequence, shown in greater detail than previous

Hitchcock murders, but in general the script allowed him to rework a number of his favourite themes – of the wrongly accused man on the run (Jon Finch) who tries to convince the young heroine (Anna Massey) that he is innocent and that she should help him. He is contrasted with the charming and likeable villain (Barry Foster) who is really a dangerous, sexual psychopath.

The picture also includes a liberal dose of Hitchcockian black humour – from the very opening scene showing a government minister at an outdoor press conference by the Thames, talking of keeping the river free of pollution, when a dead body floats into view. There is a memorable, if slightly overdone, sequence on the back of a lorry loaded with potatoes. Here the murderer struggles to retrieve a vital piece of incriminating evidence, his personal tiepin, from the hand of a corpse stiffened by rigor mortis. And Hitchcock even develops a weak comedy subplot revolving around one of his favourite subjects, food, and concerning the unfortunate police inspector (Alec McCowen) and his eccentric wife (Vivien Merchant) who insists on feeding him a variety of quite inedible gourmet meals. As Hitchcock himself recalled, 'I had a happy time with the writer of *Frenzy*. It's a crime story, but I wanted to avoid the inevitable scene among the detectives at Scotland Yard. So we had the plot points discussed by the inspector and his wife at home over meals . . .'

Appropriately enough, the main setting of the picture was the old Covent Garden market in central London. Here at one point Hitchcock contrives to track the camera back down some stairs, out the front door and into a busy street just as we realize that another murder is about to be committed. More effective by far than the murder he shows us is the one we do not see, but can only imagine. (Hitchcock makes remarkable and daring use of natural sounds, and silence, to reinforce the overall effect.)

On the whole, the picture presented a slightly uneasy and occasionally heavy-handed mixture of black comedy and suspense set in contemporary London. Though a great improvement on *Topaz*, none of the characters in the film are especially appealing, while much of the plot appears old-fashioned and uninvolving. In fact, many of these same comments could apply to his final feature, filmed four years later in California in 1975. However, *Family Plot*, as it was called, was more of a lightweight comedy-thriller, and thus avoided the most violent and distasteful excesses of *Frenzy*. Once again he worked closely with his writer, Ernest Lehman, to transform the original novel, *The Rainbird Pattern* by Victor Canning, into a Hitchcock movie. This would be his first wholly American picture since *Marnie* over ten years earlier. For

although the original novel was set in England, the subject easily lent itself to filming entirely in California – which was most convenient for a director who was not in the best of health.

It was also appropriate that for this, his very last picture, Hitchcock was able to reassemble some of the favourite members of his production team, including Albert Whitlock, pictorial design consultant and an expert on special visual effects who had previously contributed to *The Birds*, *Marnie* and *Torn Curtain*, also art director Henry Bumstead, costume designer Edith Head and Leonard South who had served as the regular camera operator for Hitch (and Robert Burks) for many years during the 1950s and 1960s and was here promoted to lighting camera-man. And there was writer Ernest Lehman who had provided the script for *North by Northwest* seventeen years earlier. It is significant that it was that long since Hitchcock had last tried his hand at a lighter weight type of thriller.

Although the plot was rather more complicated than usual with Hitch-cock, as John Russell Taylor has noted, there were actually

> two separate plots involving two separate groups of characters whose paths keep crossing; a fake medium and her taxi-driver boy-friend who are set on the trail of an heir who has vanished in childhood; and a master criminal kidnapper who is simultaneously, with the help of his girl-friend, pulling off a series of spectacularly successful jobs . . . The connection between these two strands is that the master criminal is the long-lost heir . . .

With two separate sets of characters this also made the film more economical and easy to shoot, and made it easier to do some reshooting too, when Hitchcock decided to recast the role of the lead villain: Roy Thinnes was replaced by William Devane, which pushed the cost up slightly over the original budget of $3½ million to almost twice the cost of *Frenzy*. (Since they were fairly similar productions in many respects, with a similar mixture of location and studio filming and a mainly youn-gish cast with no big star names, the comparison between them gives some indication of the difference in costs between filming in England

On location in California for the filming of his last feature, *Family Plot*, in 1975, Hitch consults with Edith Head, the doyenne of Hollywood costume designers who worked with him on many of his pictures, especially during the years following his arrival at Paramount in 1953. The winner of eight Oscars, one of her all-time favourite films was Hitchcock's *To Catch a Thief* (1955) for which she gained one of her 34 Oscar nominations.

and in California in the early 1970s.) And with both pictures doing roughly the same at the box office, it was *Frenzy* that was by far the more profitable and actually stands as Hitch's financially most successful film of his later (post-*Psycho*) years at Universal.

Interviewed by John Russell Taylor at the time that he was making *Family Plot*, Hitchcock gave some idea of the kind of balance he was aiming for: 'the way I see it, the villains are actually rather dull characters; they are the straight men, if you like; their motives are very simple and mundane. Whereas the more ordinary couple are actually very peculiar.' Without realizing it at the time, Hitchcock actually drew attention to the film's main weakness, namely, that the villainous couple are uninteresting, while the extreme contrast with the eccentric couple means that the picture does not hang together well. It certainly would have benefited from a more fully developed and convincing villain, and it is some indication of the film's weaknesses that it is effectively stolen by Barbara Harris giving a slightly quirky performance in the role of a fake medium. In other words, the comedy plot works much better than the serious one. In addition, the film seems to be unusually 'talky', with far more dialogue than one expects from a Hitchcock production.

The many setpiece sequences of note included a scene early on in which the heavily disguised girlfriend (Karen Black) collects the first ransom payment by helicopter; organized and efficient, the villain and his partner even succeed in kidnapping a bishop from in front of his entire congregation in the midst of a Sunday service. On a lighter note there is an extraordinary high angle view of a funeral and pursuit through a cemetery at one point, while most thrilling of all is the hero, Bruce Dern's, serio-comic attempt to steer an out of control car along a winding mountain road while Barbara Harris, on the seat beside him, keeps climbing all over him in sheer panic.

Fortunately, the filming was completed without any major problems during the summer of 1975 and was ready for release early the following year. Though a relatively lighweight effort, it was generally well received and was probably no more than Hitchcock was capable of, just turning 76 years old, in relatively poor health and worried over his invalid wife, Alma, who had been such a support to him throughout his long career.

In the late 1970s, Hitchcock put a tremendous amount of time and effort into one last project, 'The Short Night', loosely based on the true story of British spy George Blake and his daring escape from Wormwood Scrubs prison. But finally, in May 1979, he could no longer keep up the pretence that he was still capable of directing and closed his production office at Universal. Almost exactly one year later, on April 29, 1980, he died. Alma died two years later in 1982.

Filmography

The British Years, 1922–39

(Unless stated as otherwise, the following were directed by Hitchcock)

1922 **NUMBER THIRTEEN** (unfinished)
ALWAYS TELL YOUR WIFE (directed sequences only)
WOMAN TO WOMAN (assistant director and art director)

1923 **THE WHITE SHADOW** (art director and editor)

1924 **THE PASSIONATE ADVENTURE** (assistant director, art director and co-script)

1925 **THE BLACKGUARD** (assistant director, art director and script adapt)
THE PLEASURE GARDEN

1926 **THE MOUNTAIN EAGLE**
THE LODGER

1927 **DOWNHILL**
EASY VIRTUE
THE RING

1928 **THE FARMER'S WIFE**
CHAMPAGNE

1929 **THE MANXMAN**
BLACKMAIL (first part-talkie)

1930 **ELSTREE CALLING** (sequences only)
JUNO AND THE PAYCOCK
MURDER
MARY (German version of *Murder*)

1931 **THE SKIN GAME**

1932 **RICH AND STRANGE**
NUMBER SEVENTEEN
LORD CAMBER'S LADIES (producer only; dir. Benn W. Levy)

1933 **WALTZES FROM VIENNA**

1934 **THE MAN WHO KNEW TOO MUCH**

1935 **THE THIRTY-NINE STEPS**

1936 **THE SECRET AGENT**
SABOTAGE

1937 **YOUNG AND INNOCENT**

1938 **THE LADY VANISHES**

1939 **JAMAICA INN**

The Hollywood Years, 1939–76

Throughout most of this period Hitchcock functioned as a producer-director, though during 1940–44 in particular, there was a credited producer assigned to each of his films. He was officially credited as producer and director for the first time on *Notorious* (1946) and then on all his pictures from 1948 to 1976. Although he collaborated on the scripts of virtually all of his Hollywood films, he rarely took a story or scripting credit, as he had done on a number of his earlier, British productions, especially during the years 1927–32, often in collaboration with his wife, Alma Reville. Note, too, the Hollywood studio practice of including the head of the art department in the official credits (such as Van Nest Polglase at RKO in the early 1940s, Hal Pereira at Paramount in the 1950s). In each case these names have been included in brackets *after* the name of the art director who actually worked on the film.

ABBREVIATIONS:

prod. – produced/producer; *rel.* – release date; *phot.* – cameraman; *art dir.* – art director; *ed.* – editor; *m.* – music/score; *cost.* – costume design; *spec. effs.* – special effects; *b/w.* – black and white

REBECCA (*prod.* 1939–40, *rel.* 1940, 130 mins.)
United Artists

prod. David O. Selznick; *script* Robert E. Sherwood, Joan Harrison, adapted by Michael Hogan, Philip MacDonald from the novel by Daphne du Maurier; *phot.* George Barnes; *art dir.* Lyle Wheeler; *ed.* Hal Kern, James Newcom; *m.* Franz Waxman; *spec effs.* Jack Cosgrove; *b/w.*

Cast: Laurence Olivier (Maxim de Winter), Joan Fontaine (Mrs de Winter), George Sanders (Jack Favell), Judith Anderson (Mrs Danvers), Nigel Bruce (Giles Lacy), C. Aubrey Smith (Col Julyan), Reginald Denny (Frank Crawley), Gladys Cooper (Beatrice Lacy), Florence Bates (Mrs Edythe Van Hopper), Leo G. Carroll (Dr Baker).

A young and inexperienced girl meets, falls in love with and marries the aristocratic Max de Winter. At his country mansion, Manderley, the young bride is forced to cope with Mrs Danvers, the domineering housekeeper, and gradually discovers that Max's previous wife, Rebecca, died in mysterious circumstances. She gains a greater self-confidence, stands up to Mrs Danvers and helps Max to come to terms with the past.

FOREIGN CORRESPONDENT
(*prod./rel.* 1940, 120 mins.)
United Artists

prod. Walter Wanger; *script* Charles Bennett, Joan Harrison; *additional dialogue* James Hilton, Robert Benchley, Ben Hecht; *phot.* Rudolph Maté; *art dir.* William Cameron Menzies, Alexander Golitzen; *ed.* Otho Lovering, Dorothy Spencer; *m.* Alfred Newman; *spec. effs.* Lee Zavitz; *b/w.*

Cast: Joel McCrea (Johnnie Jones/'Huntley Haverstock'), Laraine Day (Carol Fisher), Herbert Marshall (Stephen Fisher), George Sanders (Scott Folliot), Albert Basserman (Van Meer), Robert Benchley (Stebbins), Edmund Gwenn (Rowley), Harry Davenport (Mr Powers), Eduardo Ciannelli (Krug), Martin Koslek (tramp).

An American newspaperman is sent to Europe just prior to the outbreak of war in 1939 and witnesses the apparent assassination of a leading Dutch statesman. He is followed, threatened and almost killed as he attempts to uncover the gang of thugs and Nazi sympathizers who are responsible. He is helped by Carol, an attractive young girl with whom he falls in love. Her father is finally exposed as the leader of the Nazi spy ring.

MR AND MRS SMITH (*prod.* 1940, *rel.* 1941, 85 mins.)
RKO

prod. Harry Edington; *script* Norman Krasna; *phot.* Harry Stradling; *art dir.* L. P. Williams (Van Nest Polglase); *ed.* William Hamilton; *m.* Roy Webb; *b/w.*

Cast: Carole Lombard (Ann), Robert Montgomery (David Smith), Gene Raymond (Jeff Custer), Jack Carson

(Chuck Benson), Philip Merivale (Mr Custer), Lucile Watson (Mrs Custer), William Tracy (Sammy), Charles Halton (Harry Deever).

When they learn that their marriage is not legally valid, owing to a technicality, David is amused, but Ann takes the news seriously. Incensed by his behaviour, Ann orders David out of their apartment, and he is forced to win her back in competition with a rival suitor (Jeff).

SUSPICION (*prod./rel.* 1941, 99 mins.) RKO

prod. Harry Edington; *script* Samson Raphaelson, Joan Harrison, Alma Reville, from the novel, 'Before the Fact' by Francis Iles; *phot.* Harry Stradling; *art dir.* Carroll Clark (Van Nest Polgase); *ed.* William Hamilton; *m.* Franz Waxman; *cost.* Edward Stevenson; *spec. effs.* Vernon Walker; *b/w.*

Cast: Cary Grant (Johnnie Aysgarth), Joan Fontaine (Lina McLaidlaw), Sir Cedric Hardwicke (General McLaidlaw), Nigel Bruce (Gordon 'Beaky' Thwaite), Dame May Whitty (Mrs Martha McLaidlaw), Isabel Jeans (Mrs Newsham), Heather Angel (Ethel, the maid), Leo G. Carroll (Captain Melbeck).

The young and naïve Lina falls madly in love with Johnnie, a charming, but irresponsible and penniless playboy. They elope, marry and set up house on Lina's small family income. However, she becomes increasingly distrustful of Johnnie, imagining that he is not just a charming liar, but may also be planning to murder her . . .

SABOTEUR (*prod.* 1941–2, *rel.* 1942, 108 mins.) Universal

assoc. prod. Jack H. Skirball; *script* Peter Viertel, Joan Harrison, Dorothy Parker from an original story idea by Alfred Hitchcock; *phot.* Joseph Valentine; *art dir.* Jack Otterson, Robert Boyle; *ed.* Otto Ludwig; *m.* Charles Previn, Frank Skinner; *b/w.*

Cast: Robert Cummings (Barry Kane), Priscilla Lane (Patricia Martin), Otto Kruger (Charles Tobin), Alan Baxter (Freeman), Norman Lloyd (Fry), Alma Kruger (Mrs Henrietta Van Sutton), Clem Bevans (Nielson).

A young American factory worker is wrongfully accused of sabotaging the plant where he works. He runs away, determined to prove his innocence and to capture those enemy agents who are really responsible. He becomes involved with an attractive girl whose uncle turns out to be the mastermind of the gang. He manages to uncover the other saboteurs and foil their plans.

SHADOW OF A DOUBT (*prod.* 1942, *rel.* 1943, 108 mins.) Universal

prod. Jack H. Skirball; *script* Thornton Wilder, Alma Reville, Sally Benson from a story idea by Gordon McDonell; *phot.* Joseph Valentine; *art dir.* Robert Boyle, (John Goodman); *ed.* Milton Caruth; *m.* Dimitri Tiomkin; *cost.* Adrian, Vera West; *b/w.*

Cast: Joseph Cotten (Uncle Charlie), Teresa Wright (Young 'Charlie'/Charlotte Newton), MacDonald Carey (Jack Graham), Patricia Collinge (Mrs Emma Newton), Henry Travers (Mr Joseph Newton), Hume Cronyn (Herbie Hawkins), Wallace Ford (Fred Saunders).

Uncle Charlie is welcomed by his niece 'Charlie' when he comes to stay with her family. Her suspicions are aroused that he is, in fact, a wanted murderer on the run from the police. Unable to tell her parents, even after two attempts on her life, a final dramatic confrontation between her and her uncle leads to his death instead.

LIFEBOAT (*prod.* 1943, *rel.* 1944, 96 mins.)
20th Century Fox

prod. Kenneth Macgowan; *script* Jo Swerling, John Steinbeck; *phot.* Glen MacWilliams; *art dir.* Maurice Ransford, (James Basevi); *ed.* Dorothy Spencer; *m.* Hugo Friedhofer; *cost.* René Hubert; *spec. effs.* Fred Sersen; *b/w.*

Cast: Tallulah Bankhead (Constance Porter), William Bendix (Gus Smith), Walter Slezak (Willi), John Hodiak (John Kovac), Mary Anderson (Alice Mackenzie), Henry Hull (Charles Rittenhouse), Heather Angel (Mrs Higgins), Hume Cronyn (Stanley Garrett), Canada Lee (Joe).

A group of eight survivors from a torpedoed freighter are joined in their lifeboat by a German seaman, a lone survivor of a U-boat that was sunk at the same time. An expert navigator, he is allowed on board on condition that he helps steer them to safety. But he is killed by them when they discover that he has been deceiving them into steering in the wrong direction. He was also the Nazi U-boat commander. Finally, the last six survivors are rescued.

SPELLBOUND (*prod.* 1944, *rel.* 1945, 111 mins.)
United Artists

prod. David O. Selznick; *script* Ben Hecht, Angus MacPhail from the novel, 'The House of Dr Edwardes' by Francis Beeding; *phot.* George Barnes; *art dir.* James Basevi; *ed.* William Ziegler, Hal Kern; *m.* Miklos Rozsa; *cost.* Howard Greer; *spec. effs.* Jack Cosgrove; *b/w.*

Cast: Ingrid Bergman (Dr Constance Peterson), Gregory Peck (John Ballantine), Leo G. Carroll (Dr Murchison), Rhonda Fleming (Mary Carmichael), Michael Chekhov (Dr Alex Brulov), Norman Lloyd (Garmes), John Emery (Dr Fleurot).

Dr Constance Peterson becomes involved with the new young head of an asylum shortly after he arrives. She recognizes that he is mentally disturbed and suffering from amnesia and worried that he may even be a murderer. When he flees, she follows, and together with her old friend Dr Brulov succeeds in uncovering the source of his disturbance, which leads finally to the real murderer.

NOTORIOUS (*prod.* 1945–46, *rel.* 1946, 101 mins.)
RKO

prod. Alfred Hitchcock; *script* Ben Hecht; *phot.* Ted Tetzlaff; *art dir.* Carroll Clark, (Albert D'Agostino); *ed.* Theron Worth; *m.* Roy Webb; *cost.* Edith Head; *b/w.*

Cast: Ingrid Bergman (Alicia Huberman), Cary Grant (T. R. Devlin), Claude Rains (Alexander Sebastian), Louis Calhern (Capt. Paul Prescott), Leopoldine Konstantin (Mrs Sebastian), Reinhold Schünzel ('Dr Anderson'/Wilhelm Otto Renzler), Moroni Olsen (Walter Beardsley), Ivan Triesault (Eric Mathis), Alex Minotis (Joseph).

Attracted to US government agent Devlin, the loose-living Alicia agrees to help infiltrate a gang of Nazi conspirators who have relocated in South America after the defeat of Germany. Although she and Devlin have fallen in love, when Sebastian, leader of the gang, proposes to her, she accepts. She is then able to get Devlin the information he needs, but is herself found out and made a prisoner. Devlin realizes that she is in danger and rescues her just in time.

THE PARADINE CASE (*prod.* 1946–47, *rel.* 1947, 115 mins.)
SRO (Selznick Releasing Org.)

prod. David O. Selznick; *script* David O. Selznick, Alma Reville from the novel by Robert Hichens; *phot.* Lee Garmes; *art dir.* J. MacMillan Johnson, Thomas Morahan; *ed.* Hal Kern; *m.* Franz Waxman; *cost.* Travis Banton; *b/w.*

Cast: Gregory Peck (Anthony Keane), Alida Valli (Mrs Paradine), Ann Todd (Gay Keane), Charles Laughton (Lord Thomas Horfield), Ethel Barrymore (Lady Horfield), Charles Coburn (Sir Simon Flaquer), Joan Tetzel (Judy Flaquer), Louis Jourdan (André Latour), Leo G. Carroll (Sir Joseph Farrell).

Anthony Keane, a successful young barrister in London, agrees to defend the attractive Mrs Paradine, who is accused of having poisoned her elderly, blind husband. Convinced of her innocence, Keane becomes infatuated with her, while relations with his wife begin to deteriorate. When the case begins at the Old Bailey, it becomes clear that he has mishandled his defence and misjudged Mrs Paradine. She is still in love with her valet, Latour, and confesses to the murder after Latour has testified against her and committed suicide. With his career in ruins, Keane is forced to withdraw from the case, but is consoled by his sympathetic and forgiving wife.

ROPE (*prod./rel.* 1948, 80 mins.)
A Transatlantic prod. Warner Bros.

script Arthur Laurents, Hume Cronyn from the play by Patrick Hamilton; *phot.* Joseph Valentine, William V. Skall; *art dir.* Perry Ferguson; *ed.* William H. Ziegler; *m.* Poulenc, Leo F. Forbstein; *cost.* Adrian; *Technicolor.*

Cast: James Stewart (Rupert Cadell), Farley Granger (Philip), John Dall (Brandon), Sir Cedric Hardwicke (Mr Kentley), Constance Collier (Mrs Atwater), Douglas Dick (Kenneth), Edith Evanson (Mrs Wilson), Joan Chandler (Janet).

Two young men strangle David, one of their friends, as part of a sick experiment to see if they can carry out the perfect crime. That same evening they hold an informal dinner party to which they have invited members of David's family and friends. They serve drinks from the large oak chest in which David's body is concealed. Rupert, their former teacher, becomes increasingly suspicious. He succeeds in uncovering the crime and denounces the two murderers.

UNDER CAPRICORN (*prod.* 1948, *rel.* 1949, 117 mins.)
A Transatlantic prod. Warner Bros.

script James Bridie, Hume Cronyn, from the novel by Helen Simpson; *phot.* Jack Cardiff; *art dir.* Thomas Morahan; *ed.* A. S. Bates; *m.* Richard Addinsell; *cost.* Roger Furse; *Technicolor.*

Cast: Ingrid Bergman (Lady Henrietta Flusky), Joseph Cotten (Sam Flusky), Michael Wilding (Charles Adare), Margaret Leighton (Milly), Cecil Parker (Sir Richard, the Governor),Dennis O'Dea (Corrigan), Jack Watling (Winter).

When Charles Adare arrives in Australia he becomes friendly with Flusky and his alcoholic wife, Lady Henrietta. Adare helps her to regain her self-confidence, but arouses the hostility of Milly, the Fluskys' domineering housekeeper, who is secretly in love with Flusky. When Adare is accidentally shot after an argument, Flusky faces a stiff sentence as a 'second offender'. But Lady Henrietta confesses that she, not Flusky, had shot her brother many years ago. The scheming Milly is exposed and dismissed. Adare departs leaving Flusky and his wife to pick up the pieces of their life together.

STAGE FRIGHT (*prod.* 1949, *rel.* 1950, 110 mins.)
Warner Bros.

script Whitfield Cook, Alma Reville from the novel, 'Man Running' by Selwyn Jepson; *phot.* Wilkie Cooper; *art dir.* Terence Verity; *ed.* E. B. Jarvis; *m.* Leighton Lucas; *b/w.*

Cast: Marlene Dietrich (Charlotte Inwood), Jane Wyman (Eve Gill), Michael Wilding (Wilfred Smith), Richard Todd (Jonathan Cooper), Alastair Sim (Commodore Gill), Sybil Thorndike

(Mrs Gill), Kay Walsh (Nellie Good), Patricia Hitchcock ('Chubby' Bannister).

When actress Charlotte Inwood's husband is murdered, Jonathan is suspected of the crime. He claims that he has been framed and is aided by his student actress girlfriend, Eve, who gets a job as Charlotte's dresser in order to gain her confidence. At the same time she is attracted to police inspector Wilfred Smith who is investigating the murder. By the time that Eve realizes that Jonathan is guilty she finds herself in real danger, held hostage by him, backstage in the theatre. But she manages to escape and Jonathan is killed.

STRANGERS ON A TRAIN (*prod.* 1950, *rel.* 1951, 101 mins.)
Warner Bros.

script Czenzi Ormonde, Raymond Chandler, Whitfield Cook based on the novel by Patricia Highsmith; *phot.* Robert Burks; *art dir.* Ted Haworth; *ed.* William Ziegler; *m.* Dimitri Tiomkin; *cost.* Leah Rhodes; *b/w.*

Cast: Farley Granger (Guy Haines), Robert Walker (Bruno Anthony), Ruth Roman (Anne Morton), Leo G. Carroll (Senator Morton), Patricia Hitchcock (Barbara Morton), Laura Elliott (Miriam Joyce Haines), Marion Lorne (Mrs Anthony).

Guy, a top tennis player, is travelling by train when he is approached by the shrewd but psychopathic Bruno, who proposes a perfect solution to their problems – he will murder Guy's grasping, shrewish, estranged wife, if Guy will in turn kill Bruno's father, whom he hates. When Guy's wife is murdered soon after and Guy himself is suspected, he tries to play along with Bruno. But Bruno finally decides to plant evidence that will implicate Guy in the crime, on the day that Guy is playing an important tennis match. In a race against time, Guy wins his match and arrives in

time to confront Bruno. Their fight on a runaway merry-go-round ends with the death of Bruno.

I CONFESS (*prod.* 1952, *rel.* 1953, 95 mins.)
Warner Bros.

script George Tabori, William Archibald from the play 'Nos Deux Consciences' by Paul Anthelme; *phot.* Robert Burks; *art dir.* Ted Haworth; *ed.* Rudi Fehr; *m.* Dimitri Tiomkin; *cost.* Orry-Kelly; *b/w.*

Cast: Montgomery Clift (Father Michael Logan), Anne Baxter (Ruth Grandfort), Karl Malden (Inspec. Larrue), O. E. Hasse (Otto Keller), Dolly Haas (Alma Keller), Brian Aherne (Willy Robertson).

When Otto, his sexton, confesses to Father Logan that he has killed a man, it turns out that the priest himself had a strong motive for the killing and is unable to provide an alibi for the night of the crime. Logan is indicted and goes to trial, but, bound by his holy vows, is unable to clear himself. Although he is acquitted, when Otto's wife reveals the truth, Otto flees and is shot.

DIAL M FOR MURDER (*prod.* 1953, *rel.* 1954, 105 mins.)
Warner Bros.

script Frederick Knott, from his play; *phot.* Robert Burks; *art dir.* Edward Carrere; *ed.* Rudi Fehr; *m.* Dimitri Tiomkin; *cost.* Moss Mabry; *WarnerColor* and *3-D.*

Cast: Ray Milland (Tony Wendice), Grace Kelly (Margot Wendice), Robert Cummings (Mark Halliday), John Williams (Inspec. Hubbard), Anthony Dawson ('Capt. Lesgate').

On discovering that his rich wife, Margot, has fallen for an American writer (Mark Halliday), and wishing to inherit her money, Tony decides to have her murdered. He blackmails the unsavoury Lesgate into committing what he devises as the perfect crime. But when Margot succeeds in killing Lesgate instead, Tony immediately turns this to his advantage. She is tried and sentenced for murder, but is reprieved with the help of Mark and Inspector Hubbard, who manage to trick Tony into revealing his complicity in the original murder plot.

REAR WINDOW (*prod.* 1953, *rel.* 1954, 112 mins.)
Paramount

script John Michael Hayes from the story by Cornell Woolrich; *phot.* Robert Burks; *art dir.* Joseph MacMillan Johnson, (Hal Pereira); *ed.* George Tomasini; *m.* Franz Waxman; *cost.* Edith Head; *Technicolor.*

Cast: James Stewart (L. B. Jeffries), Grace Kelly (Lisa Carol Fremont), Thelma Ritter (Stella), Wendell Corey (Tom Doyle), Raymond Burr (Lars Thorwald).

Jeffries, a news photographer, is confined to his apartment with a broken leg and passes the time observing his neighbours across the backyard. He becomes convinced that one of the residents (Thorwald), has murdered his wife and disposed of her body. Although Doyle, his detective friend, is skeptical, Lisa, his attractive fiancée, agrees to help him get the evidence he needs that Thorwald has, in fact, committed the crime. When Thorwald realizes that he is being spied on, he attacks the photographer. Thorwald is caught by the police, but not before Jeffries' other leg is broken.

TO CATCH A THIEF (*prod.* 1954, *rel.* 1955, 107 mins.)
Paramount

script John Michael Hayes, from the novel by David Dodge; *phot.* Robert Burks; *art dir.* Joseph MacMillan Johnson, (Hal Pereira); *ed.* George Tomasini; *m.* Lynn Murray; *cost.* Edith Head; *Technicolor and VistaVision.*

Cast: Cary Grant (John Robie), Grace Kelly (Frances Stevens), Jessie Royce Landis (Mrs Stevens), John Williams (H. H. Hughson), Charles Vanel (Bertani), Brigitte Auber (Danielle Foussard).

Robie, a former cat burglar, now respectable, living on the Riviera, comes under suspicion when a number of thefts are reported to the police. He is determined to capture the thief who is imitating his methods. The cool and sophisticated Francie is attracted to him and his reputation. Conviced that a lavish fancy-dress ball will attract the thief, he joins Francie and her mother at the ball and is later able to catch the cat burglar after a hair-raising, rooftop chase. Having exonerated himself he is ready to settle down with Francie (and her mother).

THE TROUBLE WITH HARRY (*prod.* 1954, *rel.* 1955, 99 mins.)
Paramount

script John Michael Hayes, from the novel by Jack Trevor Story; *phot.* Robert Burks; *art dir.* John Goodman, (Hal Pereira); *ed.* Alma Macrorie; *m.* Bernard Herrmann; *cost.* Edith Head; *Technicolor and VistaVision.*

Cast: Edmund Gwenn (Capt. Albert Wiles), Shirley MacLaine (Jennifer Rogers), John Forsythe (Sam Marlowe), Mildred Natwick (Ivy Graveley), Mildred Dunnock (Mrs Wiggs), Royal Dano (Calvin Wiggs), Jerry Mathers (Arnie).

Out hunting one autumn morning, the elderly Captain Wiles discovers the dead body of Harry in the woods and fears that he may have inadvertently shot him. It turns out that the Captain is not the only one of the local residents who has a good reason for hiding the body, including Jennifer (Harry's former wife), the artist Sam and others who think they may have been responsible for Harry's accidental death. After a farcical series of events, during which the body is concealed in a variety of ways, moved about and even buried and dug up again, it is decided that he died of natural causes. He is returned to the grove where he was first found, to be rediscovered.

THE MAN WHO KNEW TOO MUCH
(*prod.* 1955, *rel.* 1956, 119 mins.)
Paramount

script John Michael Hayes, from the story by Charles Bennett and D. B. Wyndham Lewis; *phot.* Robert Burks,; *art dir.* Henry Bumstead, (Hal Pereira); *ed.* George Tomasini; *m.* Bernard Herrmann, Arthur Benjamin; *cost.* Edith Head; *Technicolor* and *VistaVision*.

Cast: James Stewart (Dr Ben McKenna), Doris Day (Jo McKenna), Christopher Olsen (Hank McKenna), Daniel Gélin (Louis Bernard), Bernard Miles (Mr Drayton), Brenda de Banzie (Mrs Drayton), Ralph Truman (Inspec. Buchanan), Reggie Nalder (Rien, the assassin).

When Dr McKenna, his wife, Jo, and their son are on holiday in Morocco, they become friendly with a Frenchman named Louis Bernard. In the market the next day, Louis, disguised as an Arab, is stabbed by an assassin. Just before he dies he manages to tell McKenna about an assassination plot. In order to keep McKenna from telling what he knows, the gang arrange to kidnap his son, Hank. In London the assassination, which is meant to take place at the Albert Hall, is foiled at the last moment, and the McKennas manage to locate and rescue their son from the foreign embassy where he is being held captive.

THE WRONG MAN (*prod. and rel.* 1956, 105 mins.)
Warner Bros.

assos. prod. Herbert Coleman; *script* Maxwell Anderson, Angus MacPhail; *phot.* Robert Burks; *art dir.* Paul Sylbert; *ed.* George Tomasini; *m.* Bernard Herrmann; *b/w*.

Cast: Henry Fonda (Manny Balestrero), Vera Miles (Rose Balestrero), Anthony Quayle (Frank D. O'Connor), Harold Stone (Lt. Bowers), Charles Cooper (Detec. Matthews), John Heldabrand (Tomasini), Esther Minciotti (Manny's mother).

Manny, a nightclub musician, is wrongly identified as the man who has held up a number of local merchants and businesses in Queens, New York. Released on bail after being charged with armed robbery, he, his wife and his friendly, but inexperienced, lawyer (Frank O'Connor) attempt to clear his name. Fortunately, the real culprit is caught, though not before Manny's wife suffers a nervous breakdown, somehow blaming herself for the family's plight.

VERTIGO (*prod.* 1957, *rel.* 1958, 128 mins.)
Paramount

assoc. prod. Herbert Coleman; *script*; Alec Coppel, Samuel Taylor, based on the novel, 'D'Entre les Morts' by Pierre Boileau and Thomas Narcejac; *phot.* Robert Burks; *art dir.* Henry Bumstead, (Hal Pereira); *ed.* George Tomasini; *m.* Bernard Herrmann; *cost.* Edith Head; *spec. effs.* John P. Fulton; *titles* Saul Bass; *Technicolor and VistaVision*.

Cast: James Stewart (Scottie Ferguson), Kim Novak (Madeleine Elster/Judy Barton), Barbara Bel Geddes (Midge Wood), Tom Helmore (Gavin Elster), Henry Jones (the coroner), Raymond Bailey (the doctor), Konstantin Shayne (Pop Liebl).

Having resigned from the San Francisco police force, Scottie is hired by Elster to keep an eye on his disturbed, and possibly suicidal wife, Madeleine. Scottie falls in love with her, but is shattered when she apparently commits suicide. His acrophobia prevents him from stopping her jumping from a Spanish bell tower. When he meets Judy, a girl who is Madeleine's exact look-alike, he gradually discovers that he was the victim of an elaborate hoax and plot to kill the real Madeleine. His obsessive efforts to transform Judy into Madeleine end tragically with Judy's death.

NORTH BY NORTHWEST (*prod.* 1958, *rel.* 1959, 136 mins.)
MGM

assoc. prod. Herbert Coleman; *script* Ernest Lehman; *phot.* Robert Burks; *art dir.* Robert Boyle; *ed.* George Tomasini; *m.* Bernard Herrmann; *spec. effs.* A. Arnold Gillespie; *titles* Saul Bass; *Technicolor* and *VistaVision*.

Cast: Cary Grant (Roger O. Thornhill), Eva Marie Saint (Eve Kendall), James Mason (Phillip Vandamm), Jessie Royce Landis (Mrs Clara Thornhill), Leo G. Carroll (professor), Philip Ober (Lester Townsend), Martin Landau (Leonard), Josephine Hutchinson ('Mrs Townsend'), Adam Williams (Valerian).

New York advertising executive Roger Thornhill is mistaken for a government intelligence agent by a gang of enemy spies. He is almost killed, then is implicated in a murder. Forced to flee for his life, he is befriended by the sophisticated but duplicitous Eve, whom he later discovers to be the girlfriend of Vandamm, the leader of the gang. Surviving yet another attempt on his life, he learns that Eve is really an undercover agent. He then becomes involved in a plot to rescue her and capture the gang of spies.

PSYCHO (*prod.* 1959–60, *rel.* 1960, 108 mins.)
Paramount

script Joseph Stefano, from the novel by Robert Bloch; *phot.* John L. Russell; *art dir.* Joseph Hurley, Robert Clatworthy; *ed.* George Tomasini; *m.* Bernard Herrmann; *cost.* Helen Colvig; *titles* Saul Bass; *b/w.*

Cast: Janet Leigh (Marion Crane), Anthony Perkins (Norman Bates), Vera Miles (Lila Crane), John Gavin (Sam Loomis), Martin Balsam (Milton Arbogast), John McIntire (Sheriff Chambers), Frank Albertson (Cassidy), Simon Oakland (Dr Richmond), Patricia Hitchcock (Caroline).

Entrusted with $40,000 by her employer, Marion suddenly decides to steal the money and use it to start a new life with her lover, Sam Loomis. Leaving Phoenix behind, she drives to California and spends the night at a motel run by the young and likeable Norman Bates where she is murdered while taking a shower. Her sister, Lila, joins with Sam to investigate Marion's death and is almost killed herself before she uncovers the bizarre and gruesome secrets hidden in the Bates mansion behind the motel.

THE BIRDS (*prod.* 1962, *rel.* 1963, 119 mins.)
Universal

script Evan Hunter, from the story by Daphne du Maurier; *phot.* Robert Burks; *art dir.* Robert Boyle; *ed.* George Tomasini; *cost.* Edith Head; *spec. effs.* Lawrence A. Hampton; *spec. phot. adviser* Ub Iwerks; *pictorial design* Albert Whitlock; *sound consultant* Bernard Herrmann; *Technicolor*.

Cast: Tippi Hedren (Melanie Daniels), Rod Taylor (Mitch Brenner), Jessica Tandy (Lydia Brenner), Suzanne Pleshette (Annie Hayworth), Veronica Cartwright (Cathy Brenner), Ethel Griffies (Mrs Bundy), Charles McGraw (Sebastian Sholes), Ruth McDevitt (Mrs MacGruder).

Melanie, a wealthy playgirl, meets Mitch in a San Francisco pet shop. As an elaborate practical joke, the following day she drives to the Brenner family home in Bodega Bay to deliver a pair of lovebirds as a birthday present for Mitch's younger sister, Cathy. She stays on for Cathy's party. At the same time the family is concerned by strange and unexplained attacks by local birds. The attacks on the town escalate and cause havoc, while the Brenners and Melanie find themselves under siege in their house. Finally, they manage to escape in their car to an uncertain future.

MARNIE (*prod.* 1963–64, *rel.* 1964, 130 mins.)
Universal

script Jay Presson Allen, from the novel by Winston Graham; *phot.* Robert Burks; *art dir.* Robert Boyle; *ed.* George Tomasini; *m.* Bernard Herrmann; *cost.* Edith Head; *pictorial design* Albert Whitlock; *Technicolor*

Cast: Tippi Hedren (Marnie), Sean Connery (Mark Rutland), Diane Baker (Lil Mainwaring), Martin Gabel (Sidney Strutt), Louise Latham (Bernice Edgar), Bob Sweeney (Cousin Bob), Alan Napier (Mr Rutland).

When Marnie takes a job at Rutland & Co., Mark thinks he recognizes her. He is attracted to her, though he discovers that she is a compulsive thief. Instead of reporting her to the police, he virtually blackmails her into marrying him, but then is confronted with her sexual frigidity and terrifying nightmares, symptoms of her deep-seated mental illness. When he succeeds in locating Bernice, Marnie's mother, living in Baltimore, he forces Marnie to accompany him on a visit to uncover the secret of her childhood traumas as a first step to help her overcome her neuroses and start a new life.

TORN CURTAIN (*prod.* 1965–66, *rel.* 1966, 128 mins.)
Universal

script Brian Moore; *phot.* John F. Warren; *art dir.* Hein Heckroth, Frank Arrigo; *ed.* Bud Hoffman; *m.* John Addison; *cost.* Edith Head; *Technicolor*.

Cast: Paul Newman (Prof. Michael Armstrong), Julie Andrews (Sarah Sherman), Lila Kedrova (Countess Kuchinska), Wolfgang Kieling (Hermann Gromek), Tamara Toumanova (ballerina),

Ludwig Donath (Prof. Lindt), David Opatoshu (Jacobi).

When Professor Armstrong, an American nuclear physicist, apparently decides to defect to East Germany, Sarah, his assistant and fiancée, follows him on his flight behind the Iron Curtain. Armstrong is forced to kill his German bodyguard when his real mission is put in jeopardy. And he finally reveals to Sarah that he hopes to trick Professor Lindt into revealing the secret formula that he needs to complete his own work. Having accomplished this, he and Sarah manage to reach East Berlin, then are smuggled aboard a ship to Sweden and safety.

TOPAZ (*prod.* 1968–69, *rel.* 1969, 125 mins.)
Universal

script Samuel Taylor, from the novel by Leon Uris; *phot.* Jack Hildyard; *art dir.* Henry Bumstead; *ed.* William Ziegler; *m.* Maurice Jarre; *cost.* Edith Head; *spec. effs.* Albert Whitlock; *Technicolor*.

Cast: Frederick Stafford (André Devereaux), Dany Robin (Nicole Devereaux), John Vernon (Rico Parra), Karin Dor (Juanita de Cordoba), John Forsythe (Michael Nordstrom), Michel Piccoli (Jacques Granville), Philippe Noiret (Henri Jarré), Claude Jade (Michele Picard), Michel Subor (François Picard).

In 1962 at the time of the Cuban missile crisis, Nordstrom, an American intelligence agent, seeks help from a French agent (Devereux) in obtaining details of a secret treaty between Russia and Cuba. His mission takes Devereux to Cuba where he is reunited with his former mistress, Juanita, who is secretly active in the Cuban anti-Communist resistance. When her role is discovered, she is murdered. Devereux meanwhile has returned to Washington. In Paris he is reunited with his family and helps to uncover the leaders of the Communist spy ring (codename: Topaz) who have infiltrated NATO. The international crisis is over.

FRENZY (*prod.* 1971, *rel.* 1972, 116 mins.)
Universal

script Anthony Shaffer, from the novel 'Goodbye Piccadilly, Farewell Leicester Square' by Arthur La Bern; *phot.* Gil Taylor; *art dir.* Sydney Cain; *ed.* John Jympson; *m.* Ron Goodwin; *Technicolor.*

Cast: Jon Finch (Richard Blaney), Barry Foster (Bob Rusk), Alec McCowen (Inspector Tim Oxford), Barbara Leigh-Hunt (Brenda Blaney), Anna Massey (Babs Milligan), Vivien Merchant (Mrs Oxford), Bernard Cribbins (Forsythe), Billie Whitelaw (Hetty Porter), Clive Swift (Johnny Porter).

Richard Blaney is suspected of the notorious necktie murders in London when his estranged wife becomes the killer's latest victim. On the run from the police, he is helped by Babs, who is also found murdered. When he turns to his friend Rusk for help, he is arrested and realizes that Rusk is the real killer. Blaney escapes and returns to get Rusk, arriving at the scene of yet another killing. But Inspector Oxford has had second thoughts and shows up in time to catch Rusk, not Blaney.

FAMILY PLOT (*prod.* 1975, *rel.* 1976, 121 mins.)
Universal

script Ernest Lehman, from the novel, 'The Rainbird Pattern' by Victor Canning; *phot.* Leonard South; *art dir.* Henry Bumstead; *ed.* J. Terry Williams; *m.* John Williams; *cost.* Edith Head; *spec. effs.* Albert Whitlock; *Technicolor.*

Cast: Karen Black (Fran), Bruce Dern (George Lumley), Barbara Harris (Blanche), William Devane (Adamson), Ed Lauter (Maloney), Cathleen Nesbitt (Julia Rainbird), Katherine Helmond (Mrs Maloney).

Blanche, a fake spiritualist, and George, her boyfriend, set out to find the long lost nephew, and only surviving heir, of Julia Rainbird in hopes of gaining the reward of $10,000. At the same time the crafty Adamson and his partner, Fran, have been carrying out a daring series of diamond thefts and kidnappings. When Blanche and George's trail leads to Adamson, who is, in fact, the missing heir, though he doesn't know it, he becomes extremely suspicious. The couple are almost killed by Maloney, Adamson's henchman, then Blanche is held prisoner until she is rescued by George, and they are able to turn the tables on the criminal couple.

Production details of Hitchcock's Hollywood feature films

Title	Production Distribution Co.	Main shooting period	Release date	Est. cost ($m)	North American rentals	Profit/loss comments
REBECCA	Selznick International Pics/UA	Sept–Nov 39	1940	1.3	1.5	Production ran slightly over budget, but good profit
FOREIGN CORRESPONDENT	Walter Wanger/UA	Mar–May 40	1940	1.5	—	Ambitious production – small loss
MR AND MRS SMITH	RKO	Sept–Nov 40	1941	—	—	Conventional studio production – tiny profit?
SUSPICION	RKO	Feb–July 41	1941	1.25	1.8	Over budget, but earned good profit
SABOTEUR	Universal	Oct 41–Jan 42	1942	0.9	1.25	Low cost – small profit
SHADOW OF A DOUBT	Universal	Aug–Oct 42	1943	0.8	1.2	Low cost – small profit
LIFEBOAT	20th Century-Fox	July–Nov 43	1944	1.7	1.0	High cost – first serious loss-making production in US
SPELLBOUND	Selznick/UA	July–Oct 44	1945	1.7	4.7	Prestige production, but smash hit. Large ($2 million) profit
NOTORIOUS	RKO	Oct 45–Feb 46	1946	2.4	4.8	Expensive, but smash hit, large ($2 million) profit
THE PARADINE CASE	Selznick	Dec 46–Mar 47	1947	4.0	2.2	Far over budget – most expensive film – serious lossmaker
ROPE	Transatlantic/WB	Jan–Feb 48	1948	1.5	2.2	Slightly over budget – small profit
UNDER CAPRICORN	Transatlantic/WB	Aug–Oct 48	1949	2.5	1.5	Expensive Technicolor production – large loss
STAGE FRIGHT	WB	June–early Sept 49	1950	1.5	under 1m?	Moderate cost, but weak box office – small loss

Film	Studio	Shooting dates	Year			Comment
STRANGERS ON A TRAIN	WB	Oct–Dec 50	1951	—	1.8	Moderate cost, small profit
I CONFESS	WB	Aug–Oct 52	1953	—	2.0	Moderate cost, small profit
DIAL M FOR MURDER	WB	end July–Sept 53	1954	—	2.7	Moderate cost, good profit
REAR WINDOW	Paramount	Nov 53–Jan 54	1954	2.1+	5.3	Moderate cost, smash hit, large profit
TO CATCH A THIEF	Paramount	June–Aug 54	1955	—	4.5	Moderate cost, big hit, good profit
THE TROUBLE WITH HARRY	Paramount	Sept–Nov 54	1955	1.1	under 1m	Low cost, poor box office, small loss
THE MAN WHO KNEW TOO MUCH	Paramount	May–July 55	1956	—	4.4	Moderate cost, moderate hit, good profit
THE WRONG MAN	WB	March–May 56	1956	—	under 1m	Low cost, weak box-office, small loss
VERTIGO	Paramount	Sept–Dec 57	1958	2.3	3.2	Moderate cost, moderate box office, tiny profit
NORTH BY NORTHWEST	MGM	end Aug–Dec 58	1959	4.3	6.0	Expensive prestige production, big hit, large profit
PSYCHO	Paramount	end Nov 59–1 Feb 60	1960	0.8	9.0	Very low cost, tremendous hit, spectacular profits
THE BIRDS	Universal	Mar–June 62	1963	4.0	5.0	Expensive, moderate box office, small profit
MARNIE	Universal	Oct 63–end Feb 64	1964	2.0	2.3	Moderate cost, poor box office, tiny loss (?)
TORN CURTAIN	Universal	Nov 65–end Jan 66	1966	5.0	6.5	Expensive, modest box office, tiny profit
TOPAZ	Universal	June–Aug 69	1969	4.0	under 1m	Expensive, bad flop, large loss
FRENZY	Universal	Aug–early Oct 71	1972	2.0	6.5	Small cost, moderate box office, good profit
FAMILY PLOT	Universal	May–Aug 75	1976	3.8	7.4	Moderate cost, box office and profit

Notes to Table

Note that the regular pace of Hitchcock's filming from 1939 to 1960 meant that he had at least one feature film released every year from 1940 to 1960 with the exception of only 1952 and 1957. (His two most active periods of filming, in the early 1940s and mid-1950s meant that he had two films out in 1940 and 1941, also in 1955 and 1956.)

His preference for filming during the warmer months of the year (spring–autumn), followed by editing, scoring, etc., meant that his films were most often released in the calendar year following the year in which they were shot. Thus, it is worth noting that the release dates are often misleading with regard to when the pictures were actually filmed.

If inflation is taken into account, *The Paradine Case* was by far the most expensive Hitchcock production. Second place is a virtual tie between *Under Capricorn, North by Northwest* and *Notorious*. This may not be readily evident from the unadjusted figures given above. Note too that none of Hitchcock's later (post 1960) pictures is included among this highest cost group. Finally, Hitch's films have been surprisingly regular in length, particularly during the last 20 years, from 1956 to 1976. He adhered closely to a running time of about 2 hours which he appears to have felt most comfortable with. Only his two black-and-white productions, *The Wrong Man* and *Psycho*, were a bit shorter, while *North by Northwest* alone (at 136 minutes) was significantly longer.

Perhaps the most famous and best known movie director face in the history of the cinema. Hitch was a master at publicizing himself, his films and his television series. Although this portrait hints at his notoriously wicked sense of humour, there is a touch of sadness in the eyes and a suggestion of the insecurity that he suffered from throughout most of his life.

Selective Bibliography

On Hitchcock

BOGDANOVICH, PETER, *The Cinema of Alfred Hitchcock* (Museum of Modern Art, NY, 1963).

CAHIERS DU CINÉMA, issues no. 39 (October 1954) and no. 62 (August–Sept 1965).

DURGNAT, RAYMOND, *The Strange Case of Alfred Hitchcock* (Faber & Faber, London, 1974).

FREEMAN, DAVID, *The Last Days of Alfred Hitchcock* (Pavilion, London, 1985).

FRENCH, PHILIP, 'Alfred Hitchcock: The Film-maker as Englishman and Exile', in *Sight & Sound* (Spring 1985), pp. 116–122.

HARRIS, ROBERT A. and MICHAEL S. LASKY, *The Films of Alfred Hitchcock* (Citadel, Secaucus, N.J., 1976).

HIGHAM, CHARLES, and JOEL GREENBERG, *The Celluloid Muse* (Signet, NY, 1969), pp. 86–103.

HITCHCOCK, ALFRED, 'Direction', in *Footnotes to the Film* (ed. Charles Davey) (Lovat Dickson/Readers' Union, London, 1938), pp. 3–15.

LaVALLEY, ALBERT, ED. *Focus on Hitchcock* (Prentice-Hall, Englewood Cliffs, N.J., 1972).

LEFF, LEONARD J., *Hitchcock and Selznick* (Weidenfeld & Nicholson, London, 1988).

Movie magazine, issues no. 3, 6, 7 and 12, see also the *Movie Reader* (Studio Vista, London, 1972)

NOBLE, PETER, *Index to the Work of Alfred Hitchcock* – Special Supplement to *Sight & Sound* (May 1949).

PHILLIPS, GENE D, *Alfred Hitchcock* (Twayne, Boston, 1984).

REBELLO, STEPHEN, *Alfred Hitchcock and the Making of 'Psycho'* (Dembner, NY, 1990).

ROHMER, ERIC, and CLAUDE CHABROL, *Hitchcock: The First Forty-Four Films.* trans. by Stanley Hochman (Ungar, N Y, 1979), originally published as *Hitchcock* (Editions Universitaires, Paris, 1957).

ROTHMAN, WILLIAM, *Hitchcock: The Murderous Gaze* (Harvard U. Press, Cambridge, Mass, 1982).

SCHICKEL, RICHARD, *The Men Who Made the Movies* (Atheneum, NY, 1975), pp. 271–303.

SPOTO, DONALD, *The Art of Alfred Hitchcock* (Hopkinson & Blake, NY, 1976).

SPOTO, DONALD, *The Dark Side of Genius: The Life of Alfred Hitchcock* (Little, Brown & Co, Boston, 1983).

TAYLOR, JOHN RUSSELL, *Hitch* (Pantheon, NY, 1978).

TRUFFAUT, FRANÇOIS, *Hitchcock*, revised and updated edition (Simon & Schuster, NY, 1983).

WOOD, ROBIN, *Hitchcock's Films Revi-*

sited (Columbia U. Press, NY, 1989), includes the complete text of *Hitchcock's Films*, originally published in 1965, with updating and additional essays.

YACOWAR, MAURICE *Hitchcock's British Films* (Archon, Hamden, Conn, 1977).

Other Sources

BEHLMER, RUDY, ed., *Memo from: David O Selznick* (Viking, NY, 1972).

BRADY, JOHN, ed., *The Craft of the Screenwriter*, interviews with six writers, including Ernest Lehman (Simon & Schuster, NY, 1981).

CLARK, AL, *Raymond Chandler in Hollywood* (Proteus, London and NY, 1982).

FETHERING, DOUG, The Five Lives of Ben Hecht (Lester & Orpen, London, 1977).

FINLER, JOEL W, *The Hollywood Story* (Octopus, London/Crown, NY, 1988).

FINLER, JOEL W, *The Movie Directors Story* (Octopus, London, 1985, Crescent, NY, 1986).

LUHR, WILLIAM, *Raymond Chandler and Film* (Ungar, NY, 1982).

MOOREHEAD, CAROLINE, *Sidney Bernstein – a biography* (Jonathan Cape, London, 1984).

SCHATZ, THOMAS, *The Genius of the System* (Simon and Schuster, NY, 1988), see chapters 15 and 20 on Selznick and Hitchcock.

SCHOELL, WILLIAM, *Stay Out of the Shower: 25 Years of Shocker Films Beginning with 'Psycho'* (Dembner, NY, 1985).

SPADA, JAMES, *Grace: The Secret Lives of a Princess* (Doubleday, NY, 1987)

SELZNICK, IRENE MAYER, *A Private View* (Weidenfeld & Nicholson, London, 1983).

Acknowledgements

A note of appreciation to the many friends who have shared their views of Hitch with me over the years – especially Neil Hornick, who provided detailed comments on the final manuscript, also Julian Fox, Richard Chatten, Grant Lobban, Robert Stillwell and Ben Finler. Finally, a note of thanks to my patient editor, Pauline Snelson and to copy editor Robert Sneddon.

Virtually all the photographs come from the author's collection. The author and publishers would like to thank the British Film Institute Stills, Posters and Designs department for the photographs on pages 3 and 51. Almost all the photographs were originally issued for publicity or promotion by Paramount, RKO Pictures, MGM, Selznick International, 20th Century-Fox, Universal, United Artists, Walter Wanger and Warner Bros.

Index